The Plan

AuthorHouse™
1663 Liberty Drive
Bloomington, IN 47403
www.authorhouse.com
Phone: 1-800-839-8640

First published by AuthorHouse 4/12/2011

ISBN: 978-1-4490-8606-0 (sc)
ISBN: 978-1-4490-8607-7 (hc)
ISBN: 978-1-4490-8608-4 (e)

Library of Congress Control Number: 2011906076

The Plan

Unlocking God's Financial Blessing for Your Life

Meade W. Malone

authorHOUSE®

Unless otherwise identified, scripture quotations are from the King James Version of the Bible.

Abbreviations of the books of the Bible used throughout this book are adapted from the Zondervan KJV Study Bible, copyright 2002 by the Zondervan Corporation, all rights reserved, and are identified as follows:

The Old Testament:

Genesis	Gen	Second Chronicles	2 Chr	Daniel	Dan
Exodus	Ex	Ezra	Ezra	Hosea	Hos
Leviticus	Lev	Nehemiah	Neh	Joel	Joel
Numbers	Num	Esther	Esth	Amos	Amos
Deuteronomy	Deut	Job	Job	Obadiah	Obad
Joshua	Josh	Psalms	Ps	Jonah	Jonah
Judges	Judg	Proverbs	Prov	Micah	Mic
Ruth	Ruth	Ecclesiastes	Eccl	Nahum	Nah
First Samuel	1 Sam	Song of Solomon	Sol	Habakkuk	Hab
Second Samuel	2 Sam	Isaiah	Is	Zephaniah	Zeph
First Kings	1 Ki	Jeremiah	Jer	Haggai	Hag
Second Kings	2 Ki	Lamentations	Lam	Zechariah	Zech
First Chronicles	1 Chr	Ezekiel	Ezek	Malachi	Mal

The New Testament:

Matthew	Mat	Ephesians	Eph	Hebrews	Heb
Mark	Mark	Philippians	Phil	James	Jas
Luke	Luke	Colossians	Col	First Peter	1 Pet
John	John	First Thessalonians	1 Thes	Second Peter	2 Pet
Acts	Acts	Second Thessalonians	2 Thes	First John	1 John
Romans	Rom	First Timothy	1 Tim	Second John	2 John
First Corinthians	1 Cor	Second Timothy	2 Tim	Third John	3 John
Second Corinthians	2 Cor	Titus	Tit	Jude	Jude
Galatians	Gal	Philemon	Philem	Revelation	Rev

Dedication

To the Holy Spirit, who inspired me to write this book and provided the direction, prompting, insight, and revelations of scripture needed to complete it.

To my wife, Sandra; my daughter, Marisa; and my son, Timothy, for the sacrifice each of you makes daily in support of the work the Lord has given me to do. I love you all.

To my sister Barbara McDonald, for leading me into a personal and loving relationship with my Lord and Savior Jesus Christ. Who would have thought I would have gotten to know Him this way? Words cannot express my gratitude. Thank you.

To the memory of my dear loving mother, Ruth, and to my father, Randolph (Mose), for being a tower of strength in my life.

To my sister Jane Malone-Ricketts, for your prayerful and loving support of my ministry.

To the memory of my dear friend Lester Bowers, for the inspiration you have given through a life well lived in Christ Jesus.

Contents

Preface xi

Acknowledgments xiii

Introduction xv

Chapter 1
"For I know the plans I have for you ..." 1

Chapter 2
"Without me, you can do nothing" 11

Chapter 3
"Will a man rob God?" 19

Chapter 4
**"I will ... open you the windows of heaven, and pour
you out a blessing ..."** 31

Chapter 5
"He shall not destroy the fruit of your ground ..." 41

Chapter 6
**"Neither shall your vine cast her fruit before the
time ..."** 49

Chapter 7
Wait on the Lord 67

Chapter 8
"I have finished the work which thou gavest Me to do."..77

Chapter 9
Redeeming the time..87

Chapter 10
Putting it all in perspective 99

Preface

It was 2008, and I was on an American Airline flight to Barbados, reading Bishop T. D. Jakes's book *Life Overflowing: 6 Pillars for Abundant Living*, when the Holy Spirit impressed upon me to write a book titled *Unlocking God's Financial Blessing for Your Life*. As I meditated on the book's title, I was immediately taken back in vivid detail to a sermon I'd delivered, based on Malachi 3:8–12, during a weeklong revival service at the Valley Methodist Church in Tortola, BVI, earlier that year. After focusing on the sermon and its relevance to the book's title, the Holy Spirit gave very specific instructions as to how I was to conduct myself in writing it. Specifically, it was impressed upon me to write only early in the morning, with a promise that He would be there to guide me in what I would write and bring to mind the relevant supporting scriptures. After all, I had never written a book before, and I was only a lay preacher on trial in the Methodist Church. I therefore needed all the guidance I could get.

I have tried to be faithful to the initial instructions given by the Holy Spirit. Wherever I was in the world, I would arise early in the morning at the prompting of the Holy Spirit and specifically ask for His direction and guidance as I wrote. He was faithful to His promise. On those mornings when I did not feel particularly inspired by Him, I did not write a single word.

When I struggled, I would seek the encouragement of my wife, Sandra; my sisters, Barbara and Jane; and members of my prayer group, who supported me in prayer and with encouraging words.

Oftentimes, I thought that the book was taking too long to write or was concerned that it would be too short. During those times, the Holy Spirit would remind me, "Little is much when God is in it." He would also draw my attention to the books of the Bible and remind me of their individual impact on the lives of those who read and study them, despite their length. The book I was chosen to write would be one book in the body of work He has inspired and will inspire to be written to help His children successfully reach their eternal home.

During one of my trips to London, I felt led to share with my friends Ken and Gabrielle, husband and wife, and both authors, about the project. Their advice: "The title is too long. You will need to shorten it and use a subtitle if necessary." Somehow, that stuck with me. Some months later, during a family vacation in Orlando, the Lord impressed upon me the final title and subtitle of the book: *The Plan: Unlocking God's Financial Blessing for Your Life*. When I told my wife about the change, her response was, "I thought that was the title all along." That was confirmation enough for me.

Acknowledgments

Where do I begin when I know that the achievement of completing this work is a result of the total of all that has happened thus far in my life? The answer is clear. I begin with God, without whom none of this would be possible. Before the foundation of the world, He noted down in His book that I would be commissioned to write this book to the honor and glory of His name, and He organized for me a wonderful cast of loving and talented people to make it all happen. To the Lord, the author and finisher of my faith, I am eternally thankful.

To my wife, Sandra, for readily fulfilling the role of editor as identified by the Holy Spirit. May God bless you.

To Bishop T. D. Jakes, for your words of inspiration and encouragement during our meetings in the British Virgin Islands. *Life Overflowing: 6 Pillars for Abundant Living* was the initial source of inspiration for this book. Thank you and may God continue to bless you, your family, and your ministry.

To Barbara and Patrick McDonald and family, for your prayers and enthusiastic support of my ministry and all that I do. May God bless you all.

To Mrs. Else Monsanto and Reverend Tyrone Hunkins, for contributing to the editing of the book and your timely words of encouragement. Thank you.

To Dawn Gibson, for believing that I could do it from the very beginning and showing your support with action and words of encouragement. You have no idea what that meant. Thank you.

To the members of the Fort Hill prayer group, for your prayers and support of my ministry. Special thanks to Mrs. Greta Decastro, Mrs. Barbara McDonald, and Genevra Maduro for contributing to the success of the book by allowing me to share your testimonies of God's goodness in your life. May God bless you all.

To Mrs. Patricia Bowers, for willingly sharing the story of your husband's call to the service of the Lord. The inclusion of Lester's story adds an element of richness that is indescribable. Joey and Gigy, thanks for sharing your dad with the rest of the world.

To the members of the Brown's Town Prayer and Fasting Chapel, for your prayers and enthusiastic support of my ministry. You are my church family away from home.

To Ken and Gabriel, for your words of encouragement in writing the book and for your knowledgeable suggestion for the title of the book.

To the editorial staff of AuthorHouse, thank you for your guidance and editorial genius. It was just what a freshman needed.

To my brothers, Keith and Carvin, for quietly cheering me on in my ministry. I always know you've got my back. Thank you.

To my Methodist church family, thank you for your support in ministry and the role you played in shaping who I am today.

Introduction

As I reflected on God's purpose for this book, I was reminded of the passage of scripture in Exodus 12:36, where, **after doing according to the word of Moses,** God granted the children of Israel favor in the sight of the Egyptians. Specifically, the passage reveals that as the children of Israel began their journey to the Promised Land, the Egyptians lent them such things as they required. Exodus 12:35 gives us insight into some of the things that the children of Israel borrowed from the Egyptians. They included jewels of silver, jewels of gold, and raiment. As they journeyed on, God instructed Moses to "speak unto the children of Israel, that they bring me an offering: of every man that giveth it willingly with his heart ye shall take my offering" (Ex 25:2). That offering was used to fulfill the plan of God for the children of Israel to build the tabernacle and its instruments.

Scripture goes on to reveal that the offering given by the children of Israel was taken from the wealth God had granted them favor in receiving from the Egyptians (Ex 25:3–7). It was a favor God spoke of four generations previously to their forefather Abraham: "But I will bring judgment on that nation whom they will serve, and afterward they will come out with great possessions" (Gen 15:14, AMP).

When these passages of scripture are examined with an eye to learning the lessons God is teaching us about the journey each of us must take here on Earth before we reach our eternal home, they inform and instruct us on what is required for a successful journey.

As we reflect on God's word concerning the signs of the time, it is clear that our journey is close to ending. The problem for many of God's children is that they **have not done according to the word of God** and as a result have forfeited the preordained blessing and favor they require to complete successfully the plan of God for their lives. Consequently, many of God's children are at risk of not hearing the words "Well done, good and faithful servant" as they enter God's eternal Promised Land. First Corinthians 3:8 reminds us, "Every man shall receive his own reward according to his own labour." Revelation 14:13 further reminds us that our "works do follow us." Without God's favor and blessing, many of God's children have not received the resources they need to do the work God has called them to do.

Reflect for a minute on the fact that had the children of Israel not done according to the word of Moses, they would not have been granted God's favor to receive the resources necessary to successfully complete their preordained work of building the tabernacle. Reflect further with me on the fact that had the children of Israel not given their offering with a willing heart, Moses would have been obligated not to take it, and God's preordained plan for the building of the Tabernacle by the Israelites would not have been accomplished. Lastly, reflect with me on what kind of welcome the children of Israel could have expected as they stood before the Lord on that day, having not completed their assigned work.

This book will help you reflect on the fact that God has a plan for our individual lives, which includes certain works to be done. You will come away with the assurance that before the foundation of the world, God had made provision for all of the financial resources you need to successfully complete the plan. This book will help you recognize your responsibility to apply God's financial blessing to accomplishing

His plan with a willing heart. Scripture reminds us that God loves a cheerful giver (2 Cor 9:7).

It is no accident that God used the word "borrowed" in referring to the transaction between the Israelites and the Egyptians. I believe the structuring of the transaction as one between a lender and a borrower is reflective of the fact that all that we have ultimately belongs to God. As scripture reminds us, "The earth is the Lord's and the fullness thereof ..." (Ps 24:1). We are merely borrowers of what belongs to God. We are to pay back what God gives us in the way he instructs us through His holy word and the prompting of His Holy Spirit. When we grasp this fact and reflect upon it, our attitudes toward giving as the Lord directs will change dramatically.

Finally, this book will give you the assurance that God's plan has made provision to preserve and protect that which He has given to you from the adversary so that on that day, you too can hear the words "Well done, good and faithful servant ... enter thou into the joy of thy Lord" (Mat 25:23).

May God richly bless you as you explore the pages of this book, and may His Holy Spirit empower you to follow and apply His word to your daily walk until you reach home safely.

1

"For I know the plans
I have for you ..."

—Jeremiah 29:11, NIV

One of my most prized discoveries as I read and meditated on the word of God is that God has a plan for my life. On reflection, the truth of this discovery is that God has a plan for each of our lives. If you let this thought sink in for a minute, if you meditate on it for a little while, you will see how truly liberating this truth is. The God who created the heavens and the earth, the God who made man, and the God who delivered the children of Israel from Egypt with a strong hand has taken the time to design a personalized plan for my life and your life.

God has a plan for each of our lives

Over time, as the Holy Spirit led me through the word of God, I have developed an appreciation of the characteristics of His master plan for each of our lives, the understanding of which forms the foundation for unlocking God's financial blessing for your life:

- The plan was designed before the foundation of the world.
- The plan is under God's protection.
- The plan is detailed.
- The plan makes provision for a work to be done.
- The plan makes provision for all the resources necessary to accomplish it.

The Plan Was Designed before the Foundation of the World

In commissioning the prophet Jeremiah for his life's work, God said to him, "Before I formed thee in the belly I knew thee" (Jer 1:5). When we further reflect on the word of God, which records that He "rested on the seventh day from all His work which He had made" (Gen 2:2), we come to an enlightened understanding that God's plan for Jeremiah's life was made before the foundation of the world. Paul confirms this understanding in his letter in Ephesians, when he reveals that God "hath chosen us [in Christ] before the foundation of the world" and "predestined us according to the plan of Him who works out everything in conformity with the purpose of His will" (Eph 1:4, 11, NIV).

What has been even more amazing to discover is that God has recorded all the details of the plan. David, on reflecting on the awesomeness of God, said, "Your eyes saw my unformed body. All the days ordained for me were written in your book before one of them came to be" (Ps 139:16, NIV). I hope you are as excited as I am at the knowledge that the details of the plan are not to be written down or are about to be written down but that they **were written** down before the foundation of the earth. Think about it for a minute: before your mother and father ever met each other, God had already written down your name, the date of your birth, the first day of kindergarten … In fact, God had written down that you would be reading this book today in the exact location you are reading it. It is no wonder David proclaimed, "Your (infinite) knowledge is too wonderful for me; it is high above me, I cannot reach it" (Ps 139:6, AMP).

The Plan Is Under God's Protection

One of the characteristics I found particularly comforting about the plan is that it is divinely protected by God Himself. In the process of instructing his disciples, Jesus asked them this question: "Are not two sparrows sold for a cent?" Then He went on to inform them, "Yet not one of them will fall to the ground apart from your Father. So do not fear, you are more valuable than many sparrows" (Mat 10:29–31, NAS). I love this particular reference in scripture to God's divine protection because it makes clear that no matter how insignificant the detail of the plan may appear to be, or for whom the plan is designed, God is watching over it to make sure that it will be accomplished as He has ordained. His ability to do so is spoken of by Jesus himself when he said, "My Father … is greater than all …" (John 10:29).

Each of us reading this book should take comfort in the fact that the God who delivered the children of Israel from Egypt with a strong hand is overseeing every detail of the plan He has drawn up for our lives. Jesus has assured us that no devil in hell, no demon, no man, no woman, no sickness, no circumstance, visible or invisible, can stand in the way of God's plan, for He is greater and more powerful than all, individually or collectively.

The Plan Is Detailed

In the process of instructing his disciples on the meaning of discipleship, Jesus revealed, "The very hairs of your head are all numbered" (Mat 10:30). I love the fact that this verse stands all by itself. Nothing is added. It should be a tremendous source of comfort to know that the God of Abraham, Isaac, and Jacob has taken the time not only to count but to number each strand of hair on your head. Each time you comb your hair and one strand drops out, God can tell you which number it is. It then does not take a great leap of faith to conclude that God has taken care of every detail of our lives in His plan.

Jesus reinforced this point in the Sermon on the Mount, when He made known to all gathered that their "heavenly Father already knows all your needs" (Mat 6:32, NLT). What is your need today—food, clothing, shelter? Whatever your individual needs are, take comfort in the fact that God knows all about them in detail and has made provision for them in His plan for your life.

The Plan Makes Provision for a Work to Be Done

In Jeremiah 1, we read that when Jeremiah was still only a child, the word of God came to him and revealed his present and future work that had been ordained before he came out of his mother's womb (Jer 1:5). In God's overall master plan for humankind, He had carved out a work for Jeremiah as "a prophet unto the nations." What is wonderful to observe as you read about the commissioning of

Jeremiah is God's assurance that He would be with him to guide him in the things he would say and to deliver him in the time of trouble. What is also worthy of note is the clarity of the job description given to Jeremiah: "See, I have this day set thee over the nations and over the kingdoms, to root out, and to pull down, and to destroy, and to throw down, to build, and to plant" (Jer 1:10). I believe that this clear sense of direction focused Jeremiah on the things that God ordained for him to do and helped him avoid straying from the path of grace and mercy set before him.

The Plan Has Made Provision for All the Resources Needed to Accomplish It

The book of First Chronicles records King David's desire to build a house to honor the name of the Lord. However, it was not God's Plan for David that he should build His house:

> *The word of the Lord came to me ... "Thou shall not build a house unto my name ... A son shall be born to thee, who shall be a man of rest; and I will give him rest from all his enemies round about: for his name shall be Solomon, and I will give peace and quietness unto Israel in his days. He shall build [a] house for my name ... (1 Chr 22:8–10).*

What is important to note is that before Solomon was born ("a son shall be born"), God spoke to David and detailed to him the plan He had for his son Salomon, to "build [a] house [in His] name." I want you to understand that God does not plan anything or say anything that He cannot accomplish. We serve a God who cannot fail. The word of God tells us that He is watching over His word to perform it (Jer 1:12, NAS). In His plan for Solomon to build a house in His name, God made sure that all the resources necessary to accomplish it were put in place.

First Chronicles 22:14–15 provides an account of the provision David made for building the house of the Lord, including a "hundred thousand talents of gold, and a thousand thousand talents of silver; and of brass and iron without weight … timber also and stone … workmen in abundance … hewers and workers of stone and timber and all manner of cunning men for every manner of work." Indeed, all that was necessary to accomplish the plan God revealed for Solomon's life was put in place by David under the divine direction and protection of God. David acknowledged this truth before the congregation of the people when he said, "O Lord our God, all this abundance that we have provided to build You a house for Your holy name, it is from Your hand, and all is Yours" (1 Chr 29:16, NAS).

I encourage you to let the knowledge that God's plan includes all the resources necessary to accomplish the work assigned to you be a source of comfort that leads to confident action. Whatever God's assignment for your life may be, move forward today in faith, knowing that God has set in place all the people, finances, and other resources necessary to successfully accomplish it. He did it for Solomon. He will do it for you.

My family was privileged to know Reverend Lester Bowers, who on occasion would tell the story of his call to ministry. His wife Patricia (Pat) Bowers recalled him telling her that he got up one Sunday morning and put on his church clothes, as was customary, and went to the great Ebenezer Methodist Church in Antigua, West Indies. That particular morning, he had planned to attend church with some of his friends, and when he arrived, they decided to sit in the balcony.

As he sat and participated in the service, Lester reflected on the fact that he was on the verge of beginning his journey to fulfilling what he thought was his lifelong ambition of becoming a lawyer. After all, he had been accepted to law school in England and was in the process of making final preparations to leave. As he reflected, something in the sermon being delivered by Reverend Neville Brodie grabbed hold of him and awakened a lingering desire to be a youth minister.

Somehow, this dialogue between Jesus and Simon Peter by the Lake of Galilee, taken from John 21: 15–17, NLT, came alive for Lester in a way that he had never experienced before:

> *"After breakfast Jesus said to Simon Peter, "Simon son of John, do you love me more than these?"*
> *"Yes, Lord" Peter replied, "you know I love you."*
> *"Then feed my lambs," Jesus told him.*
> *Jesus repeated the question: "Simon son of John, do you love me?"*
> *"Yes, Lord" Peter said, "you know I love you."*
> *"Then take care of my sheep," Jesus said.*
> *Once more he asked him, " Simon son of John, do you love me?"*
> *Peter was grieved that Jesus asked the question a third time. He said, "Lord, you know everything. You know that I love you."*
> *Jesus said, "Then feed my sheep."*

It was as if Jesus was having a personal conversation with Lester. Jesus's piercing questions and direction to Simon Peter to "feed my sheep" gripped Lester's heart and wouldn't let it go. Jesus's words had sprung to life and added passion and purpose to Lester's desire to be a youth minister, and the road ahead for his life had become clear.

When the altar call was made, Lester was compelled to respond. He recalled that the walk down from the balcony to the altar seemed to last an eternity. That day, he was the only person who responded to the call, and all eyes and attention were on him. At the altar, he gave his life to Christ, and the journey to fulfilling God's plan for his life began.

Along the path of his journey, Lester attended the United Theological College of the West Indies and emerged as the Reverend Lester Bowers. Throughout the years that followed, this revered Methodist minister touched the lives of countless men, women, boys, and girls for Christ. Through the work God had ordained him to do as pastor, husband, counselor, accomplished tenor and friend, Lester radiated the light of Christ throughout the Caribbean and the Americas. Men saw his good works and gave praise unto Almighty God.

The path was not always easy; indeed, there were many obstacles and roadblocks along the way, but God made a way every time. Pat tells the story of his attendance at the Candler School of Theology at Emory University. Lester was given the opportunity to work part time to earn the money needed to complete his studies. However, as a foreign student, he was prohibited from working without a work visa and was told that it would be almost impossible to get it in time to accept the job and complete his studies. But that did not stop Lester. He knew that he was at Emory for a purpose, and that the God he served was faithful to complete the good work He had started.

When Lester arrived at the visa office and began to tell his story, he discovered that the person in charge of the department was a woman who attended his church in Atlanta, Georgia. Within a week, he had his visa and was able to take up the offer of employment and complete his studies at Emory. As He promised Job, God was there to deliver Lester repeatedly.

From the day he responded to God's call at Ebenezer Methodist, Lester never varied from the path of grace and mercy that was set before him. As a result, he was able to successfully complete all the days written down in God's book for him. Even though he died a young man, the essence of who he was, the lingering effects of his good works, and the evidence of lives touched by the grace of God working through him, are still very much with us today. Like a seed planted in the ground, as they are watered by those left behind, they will continue to bear fruit to the glory of God the Father.

Conclusion

As we reflect on Lester's life, we see all the characteristics of God's plan in operation. I want to assure each person reading this book that the characteristics of God's plan outlined in this chapter apply to your life. You have a personalized plan designed by God before the foundation of the world. Your plan is under God's protection; your plan is detailed; your plan has in it a work that you have been uniquely created to accomplish; and finally, your plan has provision for all the resources necessary to successfully accomplish it.

The obligation of each person reading this book is to seek out the architect of the plan through the reading of His word. He has assured us that if we seek Him we shall find Him (Mat 7:7). Our key objective in meeting with Him should be to consider carefully those things He views as critical to the successful completion of your plan. The following chapters will focus you on those things that I believe God, the chief architect, will tell you as He details the plan He has uniquely designed for you and the road you must travel to accomplish it. May God bless you on your journey.

2

"Without me, you can do nothing"

—John 15:5

In the final stages of fulfilling His divine purpose on Earth, Jesus reveals to His disciples an indisputable truth: "Without me you can do nothing" (John 15:5). I cannot impress upon you enough how important it is that each of us settles this truth within his heart, mind, and soul. If you are going to successfully live out God's plan for your life, you will need His assistance and guidance. Why? Without him your enemies, seen and unseen, are simply too strong for you.

If you are going to successfully live out God's plan for your life, you will need His assistance and guidance.

As the apostle Paul in Ephesians 6:12 reminds us, "We wrestle not against flesh and blood but against principalities, against powers, against the rulers of darkness of this world, against spiritual wickedness in high places." The Amplified Bible puts it this way:

> *For we are not wrestling with flesh and blood (contending only with physical opponents) but against the despotisms, against the powers, against (the master spirits who are) the world rulers of this present darkness, against the spirit forces of wickedness in the heavenly (supernatural) sphere.*

If we are going to complete the plan, we need God's help.

God himself confirmed to King David through the prophet Nathan: "I took thee (David) from the pasture, from following the flock, to be ruler over my people, Israel. I have been with you wherever you have gone and have cut off all your enemies from before you; and I will make you a great name, like the names of the great men who are on the earth" (2 Sam 7:8–9, NAS). God was saying to David that he was successful because of his (God's) assistance and guidance. David's response should be our response: "Who am I, O Sovereign Lord, and what is my family, that you have brought me this far?" (2 Sam 7:18, NIV). In so doing, David acknowledged that without God on his side, none of what he had accomplished would have come to pass.

I was privileged to meet Bishop T. D. Jakes in April of 2007 in the British Virgin Islands. I had seen and listened to him at a distance, but up close two things stood out from our conversations: his humility and expressed recognition of the fact that had it not been for Jesus, he would not be where he is today. Bishop Jakes further acknowledged that if God gave it to him, He could take it away at any time. He served at the pleasure of the Lord. What I took away from this giant in the faith is that he conducted himself and his enterprise in a manner that gave full recognition to the importance of God's role and the need for His continued protection, guidance, and direction.

For many of us, there is no recognition and/or acknowledgement of the need for God's assistance, protection, and guidance in our daily lives. This is evidenced by the fact that we have turned away from keeping His commandments, ordinances, and statutes (Deut 8:11). We live our lives in a manner that says to God that it is our power, our intellect, and our might that have gotten us this wealth and position in life. We have forgotten that the Lord gave us the power to get wealth (Deut 8:18). The result is that we have turned to other gods and now serve them. What gods, you ask? The gods are our houses, big bank accounts, job titles and positions, husbands or wives, and the list goes on. In the process, many have become puffed up with pride and self-importance. Indeed, many who are professed Christians are not exempt from this falsehood. As a result, they have developed a sense of godliness but deny the power thereof (2 Tim 3:5).

This is where the children of Israel found themselves a century after their return from Babylonian captivity. Ellen White's commentary on the book of Malachi observed that "their [the children of Israel] failure to fulfill their divine purpose was very apparent in Malachi's day." Put another way, the failure of the children of Israel to follow God's divine plan for their lives was evident in the way they lived their daily lives.

In Malachi 2:10, God inspires Malachi to ask this question: "Why do we deal treacherously each against his brother so as to profane the covenant of our fathers?" Malachi goes on to illustrate their treacherous behavior by referencing their growing practice of divorcing their Jewish wives of their youth to marry the daughters of foreign gods (Mal 2:11)—a practice God himself said He hates (Mal 2:16).

That same treacherous behavior exists today, as evidenced by the alarming levels of divorce among Christians and non-Christians and by the growing evidence of the fulfillment of the prophecy articulated by Paul in 2 Timothy 3:1–5, NIV:

> *But mark this: There will be terrible times in the last days. People will be lovers of themselves, lovers of money, boastful, proud, abusive, disobedient to their parents, ungrateful, unholy, without love, unforgiving, slanderous, without self-control, brutal, not lovers of the good, treacherous, rash, conceited, lovers of pleasure rather than lovers of God—having a form of godliness but denying its power.*

In the midst of the sad state of affairs that existed among the Jews, a loving, caring, and compassionate God spoke these words through His prophet Malachi: "I am the LORD, I change not; therefore ye sons of Jacob are not consumed." God goes on to lament, "Even from the days of your fathers ye are gone away from my ordinances, and have not kept them. Return unto me, and I will return unto you, saith the Lord of hosts …" (Mal 3:6–7). For each of you whom God has directed to read this book, I say to you that herein lies the secret to accessing the help you need to successfully complete the plan of God for your life.

Many of God's children, collectively and individually, have turned away from His commands and ordinances. As a result, He has turned away from them. These are His words to each of us today: "I am the LORD, I change not … Return unto me, and I will return unto you." I believe with all my heart that God will set in motion His promise of divine help and guidance that is essential in accomplishing His plan for your life.

In the midst of a sinful people surrounded by peril and crisis on every side, God spoke these words of comfort to His children:

> *Fear thou not; for I am with thee: be not dismayed;*
> *for I am thy God: I will strengthen thee; yea, I will*
> *help thee; yea, I will uphold thee with the right hand*
> *of my righteousness.*

> *Behold, all they that were incensed against thee shall*
> *be ashamed and confounded: they shall be as nothing;*
> *and they that strive with thee shall perish.*

> *Thou shalt seek them, and shalt not find them, even*
> *them that contented with thee: they that war against*
> *thee shall be as nothing , and as a thing of nought.*

> *For I the LORD thy God will hold thy right hand,*
> *saying unto thee, Fear not; I will help thee.*

> *Fear not, thou worm Jacob, and ye men of Israel; I*
> *will help thee, saith the LORD, and thy redeemer, the*
> *Holy One of Israel* (Is 41:10–14).

For those of you who turn to God for the first time, or others who have decided to return unto Him, those same words of comfort and promise of help against an enemy that is too strong for you are spoken to you today. How do you return unto Him? By accepting Jesus Christ as your personal Lord and Savior and committing yourself to following all his commands. If you would like to accept Jesus Christ as your personal Lord and Savior, say these words aloud: "I confess that Jesus Christ is Lord and Savior of my life, and I believe in my heart that God has raised him from the dead." The Bible says in Romans 10:9 that by those words spoken in faith from the heart, you are saved.

Before leading the children of Israel into the Promised Land, God spoke to His servant Joshua:

> *Be strong and courageous, that you may do according to all the law which Moses my servant commanded you. Turn not from it to the right hand or to the left, that you may prosper wherever you go* (Josh 1:7, AMP).

God's promise to Joshua for obeying His commandments is Jesus's promise to each of us today. Jesus says, "If you love me, keep my commandments. And I will pray the Father, and He shall give you another Comforter, that He may abide with you forever" (John 14:15–16). The Comforter promised by Jesus is our Paraclete, for which the Greek word is parakletos, which literally means "one called alongside to help" (King James Study Bible, page 1640). Jesus was saying to his disciples, and by extension to each of us, obey all my commandments and the Holy Spirit will be with you to help you achieve all that the Father has planned for your life. What is our responsibility? To obey his commands! Here is where we often fail. As a result, we deny ourselves of the help and resources we need to successfully fulfill God's plan for our lives.

In the book of Joshua, God commanded the children of Israel to keep themselves from the accursed thing in the city of Jericho:

> *Keep yourself from the accursed and devoted things, lest when you have devoted it (to destruction), you take of the accursed thing, and so make the camp of Israel accursed and trouble it. But all the silver and gold and vessels of bronze and iron are consecrated to the Lord; they shall come into the treasury of the Lord* (Josh 6:18–19, AMP).

One man disobeyed: "For Achan … of the tribe of Judah, took of the accursed thing" (Josh 7:1) and by his disobedience shut the door on the help and protection of God in a battle all thought they would win easily. The result was defeat. Disobedience had made the camp of Israel a curse. In their battle against Ai, a small nation they should have defeated easily, the Bible tells us that thirty-six men died, and "the hearts of the people melted, and became as water" (Josh 7:5).

In response to Joshua's lamentation before God concerning the defeat in battle, God spoke these words:

> *Israel has sinned, and they have also transgressed my covenant which I commanded them: for they have even taken of the accursed thing, and have also stolen, and dissembled also, and have put it even among their own stuff.*
>
> *Therefore the children of Israel could not stand before their enemies, but turned their backs before their enemies, because they were accursed: neither will I be with you any more unless you destroy the accursed from among you* (Josh 7:11–12).

We see that, through disobedience, the children of Israel had gone off the road that led to a successful completion of God's plan for their lives. As a result, the enemy became too strong for them. It is only after they had, in effect, gotten rid of their disobedience that God returned to them and helped them to successfully defeat their enemy. Joshua 8:1 says, "And the LORD said unto Joshua, Fear not, neither be thou dismayed: take all the people of war with thee, and arise, go up to Ai: see, I have given into thy hand the king of Ai, and his people, and his city, and his land."

I ask this question: what are the battles in your life that you believe you could win easily, but instead defeat always seems to knock on your door? Have you started a well-funded business in an area you are talented in—with talented people—but somehow it is not successful? Have you continually lost out on bids for projects you are clearly capable of executing successfully? Is the health problem you are facing progressively getting worse? Is your marriage, which started out as a fairy-tale romance, suddenly getting worse and worse despite your best efforts? I encourage you to do the same self-examination that Joshua did before the Lord and see if your life reflects one that is in disobedience to the commands and ordinances of God. If it is, I encourage you to return to God, and He will return to you with His promise of victory in the midst of your battle.

If your life reflects one that is in obedience to the commands and ordinances of God, keep the faith and keep moving forward despite the present circumstances. You serve a faithful God. His promise of help and guidance to His children in the time of trouble is sure. Remember, heaven and earth will pass away, but His word will not (Mat 24:35). In Isaiah 43:1–2, He reminds those that belong to Him:

> *Fear not: for I have redeemed thee, I have called thee by thy name: thou art mine. When thou passest through the waters, I will be with thee; and through the rivers, they shall not overflow thee: when thou walkest through the fire, thou shall not be burned; neither shall the flame kindle upon thee."*

Keep walking your deliverance is not far ahead. Say the following aloud: "Without Jesus I can do nothing" (John 15:5). "With Jesus I can do all things through Christ which strengtheneth me" (Phil 4:13).

3

"Will a man rob God?"

—Malachi 3:8

A s a newborn Christian, I remember coming across the passage of scripture in Malachi that asked, "Will a man rob God?" The passage goes on to state, "Yet you rob me. But you ask, 'How do we rob you?' In tithes and offerings." (Mal 3:8, NIV). I recalled being shocked at the revelation that I was actively robbing God in my tithes and offerings by not applying the principles to my life. What was worse was this pronouncement from God for having robbed Him: "Ye are cursed with a curse …" (Mal 3:9). I have taken that very seriously. Why? "God is not a man, that he should lie; neither the son of man, that he should repent" (Num 23:19). If He said you are cursed for withholding your tithes and offerings, it is so. The Bible tells us "heaven and earth will pass away but [His] words shall not pass away" (Mat 24:35).

I should pause for a minute and quickly tell you this view is by no means universally accepted among Christians. Indeed, among the body of believers, there is a raging debate on the question of tithing as a New Testament or an Old Testament requirement. The arguments on both sides of the debate are both persuasive and eloquent, fully supported by reference to scripture. As I reflected on the arguments, I was reminded, with a smile, of what I had heard Bishop T. D. Jakes say about tithing during one of his sermons. "I would rather have a blessed ninety percent than a cursed one hundred percent." Amen.

"I would rather have a blessed ninety percent than a cursed one hundred percent."

Foundation of Tithing

The foundation for the position I have taken lies in God's promise that was prophesied in the books of Ezekiel and Jeremiah:

> *Moreover, I will give you a new heart and put a new spirit within you; and I will remove the heart of stone from your flesh and give you a heart of flesh. I will put My Spirit within you and cause you to walk in My statutes, and you will be careful to observe My ordinances* (Ezek 36:26–27, NAS).

> *"But this is the covenant which I will make with the house of Israel after those days," declares the Lord. "I will put My law within them and on their heart I will write it; and I will be their God and they shall be My people"* (Jer 31:33, NAS).

In these prophesies, the Lord promised that He would put in our minds and write in our hearts His laws and ordinances to be administered by the Holy Spirit living in us. I believe the fulfillment of this promise under the new covenant spoken of by Paul in Hebrews 8:10: "For this is the covenant that I will make with the house of Israel after those days, saith the Lord: I will put my laws into their mind, and write them in their hearts: and I will be to them a God, and they shall be to me a people"; and re-affirmed in Hebrews 10:16, include the law of tithing, which is continually being administered by the Holy Spirit living in us.

I further agree with the commentators of the King James Study Bible, Thomas Nelson Publishers, that tithing in the New Testament serves as the minimum standard for giving. Paul, in his writing to the Corinthians, asks us to remember this: "Whosoever sows sparingly will also reap sparingly, and whosoever gives generously will also reap generously. Each man should give what he has decided in his heart to give ..." (2 Cor 9:6–7, NIV).

This transfer of the law of tithing from the old covenant to the new covenant preserves the key that unlocks the financial blessing God has provided for each of us to successfully complete His plan for our lives. For those who argue that the foundation position is not written down in the New Testament, I am reminded of the passage of scripture in Malachi 3:6, where the Lord reminds us, "I am the LORD, I change not ..." The writers of the commentary to the King James Study Bible, Nelson Publishers, on reflecting on the new covenant as prophesied in Jeremiah 31:33, further remind us: "There is in the new covenant a stress on the importance of the unchangeable principles of God's law." I agree.

Administration by the Holy Spirit

As we seek to apply the principle of tithing today, it is important to remember that God's plan under the new covenant is for His Holy Spirit to administer our giving. This is made clear through the prophet Ezekiel when God said "I will put My Spirit within you and cause you to walk in My statues, and you will be careful to observe My ordinances" (Ezek 36:27, NAS).

Paul further confirmed this in his instruction to the Corinthians when he said, "Let each one give as he has made up his mind and purpose in his heart, not reluctantly or sorrowfully or under compulsion, for God loves (He takes pleasure in, prizes above all other things, and is unwilling to abandon or do without) a cheerful giver (whose heart is in his giving)" (2 Cor 9:7, AMP).

I believe the requirement for cheerful giving from the heart can only be fulfilled continually through the divine inspiration of the Holy Spirit. Paul reported on the generosity poured out by the churches of Macedonia records:

> *Out of the most severe trial, their overflowing joy and their extreme poverty welled up in rich generosity. For I testify and that they gave as much as they were able and even beyond their ability. Entirely on their own, they urgently pleaded with us for the privilege of sharing in this service to the saints. And they did not give as we expected but they gave themselves first to the Lord and then to us in keeping with God's will* (2 Cor 8:2–5).

What is clearly demonstrated from Paul's report is a willingness to give embedded in the new heart of flesh according to the promise of

God and administered by the Holy Spirit (Ezek 36:26). It is almost incomprehensible to believe anyone giving so generously out of a state of extreme poverty without the prompting of the inspiration of the Holy Spirit.

I can recall visiting a sister in Christ during one of her visits to the British Virgin Islands. During our conversation, she told me that someone had given her a gift of one hundred dollars. Soon after she received it, she heard the Holy Spirit telling her to give the entire gift to a woman who had visited the house where she was staying. She told me she was very much in need of that money, but she was obedient to the prompting of the Holy Spirit and gave the money with a willing heart.

The woman immediately indicated her need for the financial blessing she had received and gave heartfelt thanks to God. Later that day, I had the responsibility of taking my sister in Christ to visit my parents, and we set out along what we call Ridge Road in Tortola, British Virgin Islands. As we drove, it was impressed on me to visit my brother, and we made a short detour. As we arrived and sat talking to my brother and his wife, he got up, excused himself, and went into his bedroom. On his return, he went to my sister in Christ and said, "The Holy Spirit instructed me to give you this," and he handed her four hundred dollars. *Wow!* As a result of her obedience to the prompting of the Holy Spirit, administering the laws and ordinances of God written on her heart to give to the sister in need, God fulfilled His promise that others would pour into her lap a good measure, "shaken together and running over" (Luke 6:38).

A natural question that arises is where and to whom we should give. God's word provides guidance in this area:

- Give to those who teach you the word of God.
- Give to those in need.
- Give to the household of faith.

Give to Those That Teach You the Word of God

In his writings to the Galatians, Paul instructs us, "Let him who receives instruction in the Word (of God) share all good things with his teacher (contributing to his support)" (Gal 6:6, AMP). In 1 Timothy, Paul further instructs to "let the elders who perform the duties of their office well be considered doubly worthy of honor (and of adequate financial support), especially those who labor faithfully in preaching and teaching. For the scripture says ... the laborer is worthy of his hire" (1 Tim 5:17–18, AMP).

Where are you receiving instructions in the word of God? Is it Trinity Broadcasting Network (TBN)? Is it your local church? Is it a prayer group ministry? Listen to your heart of flesh in fulfilling God's requirement to bring all the tithes into the storehouse and give as the Holy Spirit prompt you in your heart to give.

Give to Those in Need

In writing to the Ephesians, Paul's exhortation to them was to "Let the thief steal no more, but rather let him be industrious making an honest living with his own hands so that he may be able to give to those in need" (Gal 4:28, AMP). Indeed, as the Psalms remind us, "Blessed is he that considereth the poor: the LORD will deliver him in time of trouble. The LORD will preserve him, and keep him alive; and he shall be blessed upon the earth: and thou wilt not deliver him unto the will of his enemies" (Ps 41:1–2).

Wherever you are in the world today, the number of those in need appears to be growing daily. As the Holy Spirit directs you in this area, give confidently, knowing that the Lord has made provision for your reward in His word. The Gospel of Luke further encourages us to give and it shall be given unto you. They will pour into your lap a good measure pressed down, shaken together, and running over. For by your measure, it will be measured to you in return (Luke 6:38, NAS).

Give to the Household of Faith

In Paul's letter to the Philippians, he writes, "You Philippians know, in the early days of your acquaintance with the Gospel when I set out for Macedonia, not one church shared with me in the matter of giving and receiving, except you only; for even when I was in Thessalonica, you sent me aid again and again when I was in need" (Phil 4:15–17, NIV). The Philippians act of generosity in supporting Paul's ministry was not without its blessing, for Paul confidently declared to the Philippians, "God will supply all your needs according to His riches in glory by Christ Jesus" (Phil 4:19).

An example of the manifestation of Paul's declaration can be found in the story of the widow of Zarephath, found in 1 Kings 17:9–16. In this story, in the midst of a severe famine, the widow was prompted to give to the man of God (Elijah) all that she had left to feed her and her son. Because of her obedience to the prompting of the Holy Spirit to give selflessly to Elijah, God poured out a blessing and supplied her household's need for food until the famine ended. He will do the same for you.

Tithing Is the Key

On reflection, the major obstacle for many Christians in embracing God's commands in the area of tithing is not the theological arguments for or against the principle but a lack of knowledge and faith, the cost of which is immeasurable. The prophet Hosea reminds us that God's people are destroyed for lack of knowledge. Some have gone as far as rejecting the knowledge of God's laws and commands, and as a result, God has rejected them (Hos 4:6). Those that have knowledge but lack faith in His word are no better off. Paul reminds us that without faith, without an uncompromising belief in His word, it is impossible to please God (Heb 11:6, AMP). We could go on for chapters on the subject of faith, but my simple response to the word of God is this: If God said it, I believe it and act upon it in faith. Why? God cannot lie. He is truth; If He said it, it is already established in accordance with His divine purpose and will.

God's people are destroyed for lack of knowledge

With God's truth established, let's explore together this key of tithing and offering and its impact on the financial blessing God has planned for your life. In God's overall plan for tithing and offering, He has made provision for a curse and for a blessing. What is critical for us to understand is that God's pronouncement of curse or blessing is not simply a result of our tithing or not tithing. It is a result of our ongoing obedience or disobedience to His command for us to tithe.

Leviticus 27:30 reminds us: "All the tithe of the land … is the Lord's; it is holy unto the Lord." No wonder God says to the children of Israel,

"Ye have robbed Me"; the tithe belongs to Him. He has claimed it as Holy unto Himself. It is consecrated unto the Lord.

By our disobedience to the command of the Lord to tithe, many of us have taken for ourselves what belongs to God and placed it among our own stuff. Consider again what the Lord said concerning Achan's trespass in taking of the things that were ordained to be consecrated unto the Lord. "Israel has sinned; they have violated my covenant, which I commanded them to keep. They have taken some of the devoted things; they have stolen, they have lied, they have put them with their own possessions" (Josh 7:11). God's declaration for our theft of His tithes and offerings: "Ye are cursed with a curse: for ye have robbed Me ..."

Leviticus 26:14–17, NIV, gives us an indication of the curse spoken of by the Lord:

> *But if you will not listen to me and carry out all these commands, and if you reject my decrees and abhor my laws and fail to carry out all my commands and so violate my covenant, then I will do this to you: I will bring upon you sudden terror, wasting diseases and fever that will destroy your sight and drain away your life. You will plant seed in vain, because the enemies will eat it. I will set my face against you so that you will be defeated by your enemies; those who hate you shall rule over you, and you will flee even when no one is pursuing you.*

As we pause to consider what God has said, it is important for us to reflect on the fact that **all** we have or hope to gain belongs to God. As we are reminded in His word, "The earth is the Lord's and the fullness thereof ..." (Ps 24:1). Our God is already rich in houses and land. He is already the owner of the cattle on a thousand hills (Ps 50:10). Let's not fool ourselves; God is not waiting in heaven for us to give Him anything. It is already His, all of it. David acknowledged this truth in 1 Chronicles 29:12, where he said, "Both riches and honour come from thee ..." The giving of our tithes and offerings is therefore an act of obedience to the command of God. When we give it willingly as an act of worship and acknowledgement of God's sovereignty over our lives and all that we own, God's response, according to His word, is to open up the windows of heaven and pour us out a blessing, that there will not be room enough to receive it (Mal 3:10). Put another way, our tithing as an act of worship and reverence to God is the key that unlocks the door of God's financial blessing prepared for each of us before the foundation of the world. That blessing is the source of all the resources you will need to successfully complete God's plan for your life.

---

our tithing as an act of worship and reverence to God is the key that unlocks the door of God's financial blessing

---

In Malachi 3, God challenges the children of Israel to prove Him in His promise to bless them once they have obeyed His command to tithe. I challenge you today to test Him. As the Holy Spirit prompts you to be obedient to the command of God to tithe, give as you have made up in your mind to give and purpose in your heart not reluctantly or sorrowfully or as under a compulsion of the law to give but with a cheerful heart (2 Cor 9–7). I am confident that the God who never changes will fulfill His promise of blessing in your life.

I end with a testimony from a sister in Christ, at our Fort Hill Prayer

Group, who simply blessed my heart and encouraged all who heard it. She testified that she once had little money in her bank account and was in line at the bank to deposit some money. Out of nowhere, a friend she had not seen for a long time showed up. During their conversation, he shared with her that his business was doing well and encouraged her to tithe 10 percent of her income from her business to the church. He further encouraged her that if she did this, she would see how the windows of heaven would open and bless her business.

The sister shared that after she heard the story, she felt guilty because she was not practicing the principle of tithing and wondered if that was the reason her business was not doing well. On reflection, she remembered that she was due to collect a check of five thousand dollars from a catering job she had just completed, and she pledged immediately to deduct 10 percent and seed it to the church. As promised to God, when she received the check, she took out the 10 percent and gave half to her sister to seed in her church, and she seeded the other half in her church. Immediately, the Lord opened the windows of heaven and began to pour out His blessing on her:

- On Monday, October 4, 2010, she was offered a monthly catering job for a company from October 2010 to September 2012—a two-year assignment.

- On Tuesday, October 5, 2010, she was offered a catering job for fifty persons.

- On Wednesday, October 6, 2010, she received confirmation that she would be doing a catering job for four hundred persons in December.

- On Thursday, October 7, 2010, she was offered two catering jobs for forty and thirty persons, respectively.

- On Friday October 8, 2010, she was offered a catering job for eighty persons.

My Sister in Christ concluded her testimony with these words: "This test has taught me how to take God at His word and be obedient unto it. I have found out that if we do not follow His word, we will miss our blessing that is awaiting us." Amen!

I pray that as you read this testimony, you too are encouraged and determined in your heart to allow the Holy Spirit to administer God's statutes concerning tithing so that He may fulfill His promise of abundant blessing in your life. What he did for my sister in Christ, he will do for you.

4

"I will ... open you the windows of heaven, and pour you out a blessing ..."

—Malachi 3:10

A Natural question that emerges is how does God manifest His blessing? The response is through our faith in the promise of God. This is His promise. If you bring your whole tithe into the storehouse ... He (God) will open the windows of heaven and pour you out a blessing until it overflows (Mal 3:10, NAS). The challenge for each of us as we commit ourselves to the principle of tithing is to live out our faith in the promise of God in the face of an everyday reality that does not yet reflect the manifestation of His Promise.

Many of you reading this book have diligently committed yourselves to the principle of tithing, but your everyday reality may be far from one overflowing with blessing. My immediate encouragement to you is to keep the faith and keep moving forward. We serve a faithful

God who has the power to deliver on every promise He has made. Remember, the manifestation of God's blessing is often behind our test of faith in His promise.

We serve a faithful God

This was the case with Abraham (formerly Abram), the father of our faith. In Genesis 12, we learn of the commissioning of Abraham to leave his father's house to go to a land that God would show him with this promise:

> *And I will make of thee a great nation, and I will bless thee, and make thy name great; and thou shall be a blessing:*
>
> *And I will bless those that bless thee and curse those that curseth thee: and in thee shall all the families of the earth be blessed* (Gen 12:2–3).

The Lord was saying to Abraham to do as He commanded thee, and that He would pour him out an overflowing blessing. The challenge for Abraham was to live out his faith in the promise of God in the face of his every day reality, which did not reflect the complete manifestation of God's promise, even though he had fulfilled the principle of tithing by giving a "tenth of everything" to Melchizedek, "priest of the God Most High" (Gen 14:18–20, NIV).

Ten years after God had made the promise of making Abraham a great nation, Abraham's wife, Sarah, had not yet bore him a child (Gen 16:1–3). The level of Abraham's frustration as a human being living out the reality of his circumstance is seen in his response to

God after receiving verbal confirmation of His promise. "O Sovereign Lord, what can you give me since I remain childless and the one who will inherit my estate is Eliezer of Damascus? … You have given me no children: so a servant in my household will be my heir" (Gen 15:2–3, NIV).

From a human perspective, it is not a surprise that Abraham, the father of faith, gave into his wife's offer to take Hagar, her maid, to be his wife. Abraham went in unto Hagar, and she conceived (Gen 16:4). Immediately, all hell broke lose in Abraham's household. His wife, Sarah, said unto him, "My wrong is upon thee. I have given my maid unto thy bosom and when she saw that she had conceived I was despised in her eyes …" (Gen 16:5).

If we are truthful, the fact is that Abraham's story is not unlike our own. For many of us, our temporary lapses of faith in the midst of everyday realities that reflect the yet unfulfilled promises of God have resulted in us stepping outside the plan of God for our lives, only to discover that it was the wrong decision.

I believe that what Sarah and Abraham failed to do, in that moment, was to ground their faith in the blessings God was already pouring into their lives: blessings that would serve as the foundation for the successful fulfillment of His promise.

God had promised Abraham that He would bless him, and indeed there is good evidence that Abraham was being blessed. In the midst of a famine, Abraham went down to Egypt and, by the divine intervention of God, came back a man described as "very rich in cattle, in silver, and in gold" (Gen 13:2). Later on, we again see the Lord's divine intervention with Abimelech, king of Gerar, resulting in Abraham receiving "sheep, and oxen, and menservants, and womenservants … and land to dwell in … and a thousand pieces of silver" (Gen 20:14–16).

God had also promised Abraham that He would make his name great, and there is every indication that God had begun that process. In the battle to rescue Lot, his nephew, God had made him victorious with only three hundred and eighteen of his trained servants, over the armies of four kings, who had earlier defeated the armies of Sodom, Gomorrah, Admah, Zabolim, and Zoar (Gen 14:1–15). The evidence of God's role in the victory and the elevation of Abram in the site of the defeated kings was declared by Melchizedek, the priest of the most high God, saying: "Blessed be Abram of the most high God, possessor of heaven and earth: And blessed be of the most high God, which hath delivered thine enemies into thy hand …" (Gen 14:19–20).

We later see King Abimelech saying of Abraham, "God is with thee in all that thou doest" (Gen 21:22) and the sons of Heth addressing him as "my lord" and declaring that he was "a mighty prince among them" (Gen 23:6). Indeed God was fulfilling His promise to Abraham, not only to his generation but for all generations to come as well.

God had further promised Abram that He would bless those that blessed him and curse those that cursed him. During Abraham's individual journey to Egypt and Gerar, we see the manifestation of God's promise to curse those who curse him. Because of Pharaoh and King Abimelech's decision to take Sarah as their concubine, God fulfilled His promise and cursed each king. In the case of Pharaoh, Genesis 12:17 states, "The Lord plagued Pharaoh and his house with great plagues because of [Sarah, Abraham's wife]." In King

Abimelech's case, God caused the wombs of his entire household to be closed up because of Sarah, Abraham's wife (Gen 20:18).

God's promise of blessings for those who blessed Abraham was also activated in King Abimelech's case. God had pronounced him a dead man for having taken Abraham's wife (Gen 20:3). However, God further communicated to Abimelech that if he should restore unto Abraham his wife, he shall pray for him and he shall live (Gen 20:7). As a result of Abimelech's obedience to the instructions of the Lord in restoring unto Abraham his wife, Sarah, and his blessing of Abraham with sheep, and oxen, and menservants, and womenservants, God blessed him according to His promise to Abraham: "So Abraham prayed unto God: and God healed Abimelech, and his wife, and his maidservants; and they bare children" (Gen 20:14 and 17).

As you live out the reality of your daily life and wait for the complete manifestation of His promise, I encourage you to step back and reflect on the blessings God is already pouring into your life. It may be that you have begun to enjoy good health that allows you to go to work each day. It may be that your children are finally doing well in school or in their careers. It may be that you are now enjoying a supportive relationship with your spouse, which is allowing you to pursue a lifelong dream. It may be that the friendships that God allowed you to develop are a source of blessing. It may be that you are particularly gifted in certain areas and finally have the resources to develop your talents.

Whatever your blessing may be, I encourage you to strengthen your faith in all that God has done and is doing rather than overreacting to those aspects of the plan that have not yet manifested. Celebrate your blessings by giving God thanks and praise. Remember, "He who began a good work in you will carry it on to completion until the day of Christ Jesus" (Phil 1:6, NIV).

Indeed, that was God's encouragement to Abraham:

> *I will make my covenant between me and thee, and I will multiply thee exceedingly ... and thou shalt be a father of many nations ... and I will make nations of thee, and kings shall come out of thee* (Gen 17:2–6).

God was saying to Abraham that even though he did not yet see the manifestation of all that He had promised him, it would surely happen. He was saying that he had planned for his life all that he had spoken of before the foundation of the world, and He had the power to make it a reality, for He is the God of all flesh, and there is nothing too hard for Him (Gen 18:14). Scripture reveals that Abraham "believed in the Lord" (Gen 15:6).

In the fullness of time, the Bible records the following:

> *The Lord visited Sarah as He had said, and the Lord did unto Sarah as He had spoken. For Sarah conceived, and bare Abraham a son in his old age, at the set time of which God had spoken to him. And Abraham called the name of his son that was born unto him, whom Sarah bare to him, Isaac* (Gen 21:1–3).

Finally, at the age of one hundred, twenty-five years after the initial promise was made, Abraham, through his faith in the promise of God, was able to celebrate the manifestation of God's promise, and "Abraham made a great feast the same day that Isaac was weaned" (Gen 21:8).

Indeed the foundation was now complete for making the nations God promised He would make of Abraham (Gen 17:6). Abraham's role would be to put his faith in action by obeying the voice of the Lord, in spite of the perceived challenges, in order to establish that which God had promised. In Genesis 26, we see confirmation of Abraham's obedience to God's commandments:

> *And the Lord appeared unto him (Isaac) and said, "I will make thy seed to multiply as the stars of heaven, and will give unto thy seed all these countries; and in thy seed shall all the nations of the earth be blessed; because that Abraham obeyed my voice, and kept my charge, my commandments, my statues, and my laws (Gen 26:2–5).*

I want to remind you of these truths: "God is not a respecter of persons" (Acts 10:34). However, He is a respecter of His word. He has proclaimed, "Heaven and earth will pass away: but My words will not pass away" (Luke 21:33). As you live your lives in obedience to His command to bring all your tithes into the storehouse, under the administration of the Holy Spirit, you must exercise your faith in the promise of God to pour out your blessing from the windows of heaven. Start the journey knowing that before the foundation of the world was laid, God had already established your blessing, and He will release it at the right time as you exercise your faith in His promise through your actions. It will take courage and strength, but remember that with Him, all things are possible.

I can recall when God made a way for my family to purchase the British Virgin Islands practice of PricewaterhouseCoopers. There was no money in sight for accomplishing the transaction. In thinking through how I would purchase the firm, God brought to mind a gentleman who, over the years, had become a friend and was at the time CEO of a major banking institution outside of my country. With no money of my own to purchase the firm, I prepared a financing proposal to present to him for consideration. I vividly remember the day I arrived at the bank. He had made arrangements for my accommodations and invited me to have lunch in the bank's private dining room. I sat and made my presentation to his senior lending officer, who had joined us for lunch. To my surprise, at the conclusion of lunch, my friend said these words: "Before the afternoon is past, you will have a term sheet in your hands." I went back to the hotel and waited. True to his words, before the end of the day, in less than three hours, I had a term sheet, which provided for the finances I would need to purchase the firm (glory be to God).

After receiving the term sheet from the bank, I traveled back to the British Virgin Islands, still filled with fear about my ability to complete the transaction. While driving home, in the midst of my doubt, the Holy Spirit spoke to me in a firm yet loving tone: **"What must I do to convince you that I am with you?"** Immediately, my attitude changed, and faith replaced the lingering doubt and fear within me.

Not long after, I traveled to London to complete the negotiations for the purchase of the firm. Those negotiations were far more difficult than I could have ever imagined. Instead of being accommodating because I was a partner in the firm, my fellow partners were very commercial and demanded a price above the amount that the bank had provided for in the term sheet. I left those negotiations feeling disappointed but not defeated. The words the Holy Spirit had spoken to me earlier provided comfort and a quite assurance that all was well. I further encouraged myself with the fact that a fixed price was established, and once funding was secured, my family and I would own the firm.

I went back to the British Virgin Islands and told the young man who was secretly assisting me what had happened. Together we worked on the financial projections and proposal for the additional funding needed to purchase the firm. Then came the decisive moment. I remember calling my friend on the phone and telling him about the negotiations. He listened quietly and then responded in a fatherly manner, "We will give you the additional money you need to complete the transaction." I was overjoyed and filled with thanksgiving for what the Lord had done.

Through faith in the promise of God that He was with me on the journey to purchase the firm, together with my actions in support of my faith, I was able to receive God's overflowing blessing. He will do the same for you. Start up your faith engine today and begin your journey. I am confident that the God we serve will richly bless you along your way.

5

"He shall not destroy the fruit of your ground ..."

—Malachi 3:11

Ask any farmer and he will tell you that before you can reap fruit of any kind, you must start by planting a seed in the ground. No seed, no fruit. Our thoughts are equivalent to the seed. If we reflect for a minute, we will quickly conclude that nothing in our lives is ever accomplished without it first being conceived in our thoughts. Think about it for a second—everything we do begins with a thought. It is through our thoughts that God directs us along the pathway of His plan for our lives by planting "seeds of thought" in our minds, which lead to the formulation of plans and actions and ultimately to the completion of God's plan.

---

*It is through our thoughts that God directs us
along the pathway of His plan for our lives*

The "planter" of God's seeds of thought in each of our minds is the Holy Spirit. In John 16, Jesus counsels His disciples about the work of the Holy Spirit, who would come after He goes away, saying the following:

> *When the Spirit of Truth comes, He will guide you into all the truth; for He will not speak of His own, but will speak whatever He hears, and will declare to you the things that are to come. He will glorify Me, because He will take what is mine and declare it to you. All that the Father has is mine. For that reason I said that He will take what is mine and declare it to you* (John 16:13–15, NRSV).

The guidance provided by the Spirit of Truth in this passage of scripture is accomplished through your thoughts. The Holy Spirit, upon hearing from Jesus, plants seeds of thoughts in your mind and then nurtures and protects them until they manifest into actions that will lead you to the fulfillment of God's plan for your life.

A natural question that emerges is how to know which of your thoughts are being planted by the Holy Spirit. This passage from John 16 provides a filter through which you can test your thoughts to see if they are of God. This filter is activated through two questions that you must continually ask yourself as you process the thoughts that come into your mind:

- Does it line up with the word of God?
- Does it glorify Jesus?

If any of your thoughts fail any of these two tests, they are not from God.

Does It Line up with the Word of God?

The passage of scripture from John 16 reminds us that the Holy Spirit "will not speak on His own, but will speak whatever He hears." The person from whom the Holy Spirit hears what He speaks is Jesus. For Jesus said, "He will take what is mine and declare it to you." Jesus goes on to say, "All that the Father has is mine. For this reason I said that He will take what is mine and declare it to you" (John 16:14–15).

Jesus was being careful not to cause any confusion among His disciples, or anyone who would follow Him, by clarifying that all that the Father has belongs to Him. One of the truths that comes out of this declaration is the fact that every word spoken by God belongs to Jesus, and every word spoken by Jesus belongs to God. There is no division among them. By extension, every word spoken by the Holy Spirit is from the same source.

Jesus was also looking ahead and preparing His disciples to believe and act upon whatever the Holy Spirit would say to them, irrespective of whether it could be identified with Him or His Father. We must also do the same.

The tool given to us to confirm the origin of the voice speaking to us and the thoughts that come into our minds is the Holy Bible. Second Timothy 3:16 reminds us that every word written in the Bible is through the inspiration of the Holy Spirit. Every time one of the authors of the Bible sat down to write, the Holy Spirit provided him with the words, the sentence structure, the complete thought provided in each paragraph, the stories, the references, and the conclusion for every chapter. In so doing, God made sure that everything that He would say to us and every thought that He would plant in our minds through the Holy Spirit could be found and supported in the Bible.

When you hear a voice speaking or a thought pops into your mind, test its origin through the word of God. If you cannot find it in the Bible or support it through scripture, then you know it is not from God.

As a newly born Christian, I remember attending a youth week event under the leadership of Pastor Calvin Mills and one of our youth leaders in our Methodist church. During their presentations, both of them kept referring to conversations with the Lord. After some time listening, I finally got the courage to ask, "How do you know you're speaking with God? Pastor Mills's simple response was revolutionary to me. He said, "You know you are speaking with God if you can find what He is saying in the Bible. If your conversation fails this test, you know for certain that God is not speaking."

Every day, as thoughts come to your mind, you need to filter them through the word of God. If they do not pass the test, cast them out. Do not let them form root by pondering them or actively pursuing them. They are not part of God's plan for your life. They will often lead to failure, stress, worry, disappointment, or worse yet, destruction. They are works of the devourer who has come to steal, kill, and destroy (John 10:10).

If your thoughts pass the test and line up with the word of God, one more test must be passed before you proceed: Does it glorify Jesus?

Does It Glorify Jesus?

The Holy Spirit's work in our lives is to point us to Jesus and to bring Glory to His Name. Jesus declared of the Holy Spirit, "He will bring glory to Me by taking from what is mine and making it known to you" (John 16:14, NIV).

Every thought that is inspired by the Holy Ghost working in you **will** ultimately bring glory to Jesus. Don't be fooled. If the thought and the actions that will naturally follow do not glorify Jesus, it is not of God. He declared in Isaiah 48:11, "I will not give My glory unto another." Glory belongs to Jesus. If your actions will ascribe glory to you, stop! It is not from God.

Many people, including Christians, are led astray by thoughts that on the surface pass the first test but on inspection fail the second test. If pursued, they will not glorify Jesus. Oftentimes, the pursuit of those thoughts are grounded in pride and seek to bring recognition to oneself. We must guard against these thoughts and reject giving them power by our actions. Remember, the Bible encourages you to "cast down imaginations and every high thing that exalteth itself against the knowledge of God, and bring into captivity every thought to the obedience of Christ (2 Cor 10:5).

Ask yourself the tough question and be honest with yourself about the response you receive. Is it all about Jesus? Or is it about you or someone else? God will give you an answer if you seek Him out earnestly through prayer or fasting. His response to you may come through the reading or hearing of His word—or it may be through a vision or a dream. Your response will often come through a quite peace in your spirit that lets you know that what you are contemplating is of

God. If it is not of God, you will often have uneasiness in your spirit or nervousness about pursuing the actions that would be required to bring the thought to a successful conclusion.

If after some seeking, you are still unsure, particularly for big decisions such as moving, selling a house, changing careers, and so forth, I encourage you to seek out a man or woman of God and share your thoughts with that person. How will you know whom to go to? The Bible tells us we shall know them by their fruits (Mat 7:16). If someone is living a life that lines up with the word of God and the power of God is being manifested in his life, then you have the right person.

If you feel that you cannot share your thoughts with a man or woman of God, then you know immediately that your thoughts are not of God. Why? God is light. Everything that is of Him can be shared openly with His saints. If you have liberty to share with a man or woman of God and your thoughts and the actions that would naturally follow are of God, I believe that his spirit will bear witness with your spirit and convince you that you have heard from God. Remember that Jesus has made provision in His word for the agreement of two to manifest His power (Mat 18:19).

In Acts, we learn this about Paul and Silas:

> *They passed through the Phrygia and Galatia region, having been forbidden by the Holy Spirit to speak the word in Asia; and after they came to Mysia, they were trying to go into Bithynia, and the Spirit of Jesus did not permit them; and passing by Mysia, they came down to Troas. A vision appeared to Paul in the night: a man of Macedonia was standing and appealing to him, and saying, "Come over to Macedonia and*

help us." When he had seen the vision, immediately we sought to go into Macedonia, concluding that God had called us to preach the gospel to them (Acts 16:6–10, AMS).

From the recount of Paul and Silas's journey, it is important to note that Paul and Silas's desire to speak the word of God in Asia passed the first test: it lined up with the word of God. After all, it was Jesus himself who commissioned His disciples to "go into all the world and preach the gospel to every creature" (Mark 16:15). However, it was not God's will for them to preach in Asia at that time. To pursue that thought by their actions, no matter how well intentioned on the surface, would not glorify Jesus.

God's plan for their lives called for them to go to Macedonia to proclaim the good news to the people there. To communicate His plan, God spoke through a vision given to Paul of a man of Macedonia pleading with him to come over and help. Paul and Silas's response was to cross over to Macedonia immediately, convinced that it was God's will that they go.

Indeed, despite the suffering Paul and Silas endured, Jesus was glorified in Macedonia. The book of Acts records that after Paul and Silas had been released from prison by the miraculous power of God, the keeper of the prison brought them out and said:

Sirs, what must I do to be saved? They answered, Believe on the Lord Jesus, and you will be saved, you and your household. They spoke the word of the Lord to him and to all who were in his house. At the same hour of the night, he took them and washed their wounds; then he and His entire family were baptized without delay. He brought them up into the house and set food before them; and he and his entire household rejoiced that he had become a believer in God (Acts 16:30–34).

While it would have been clear to Paul that the words spoken to him in the vision lined up with the word of God, I believe that he became convinced thorough the sharing of his vision with Silas. During that dialogue, I believe the Holy Spirit bore witness with Silas's spirit that the vision Paul was sharing was from God, and he was able to agree with Paul to go to Macedonia.

Paul and Silas's story is a perfect example of denial of oneself for the glory of God. As they walked toward Macedonia, I believe they did so with an extra pep in their steps, knowing that God was with them and all would be well. After all, they were on a mission from God, and they could not fail. Everything they needed for a successful outcome was already provided.

The same is true for you and me. Test the voice that speaks to you and the thoughts that come into your mind through the Bible. If it passes that test, make sure that your actions that will naturally follow will bring glory to Jesus. If you receive confirmation, then move forward with confidence, knowing that God is with you and no devil in hell, no matter how powerful, will stop you from bringing glory to Jesus as you achieve God's plan for your life.

6

"Neither shall your vine cast her fruit before the time ..."

—Malachi 3:11

Attacks on the Seed

After a seed is planted, its ability to survive and grow will depend on how well the farmer has prepared the soil and the effectiveness of his intervention in the event of an attack on the seed. The same is true for your "seeds of thought" planted in your mind by the Holy Spirit. Once you have tested your thoughts and they pass the tests, your immediate challenge will be to protect your "seeds of thought" against the devourer.

Your preparation and defense against the attacks should be twofold. Number one is accepting Jesus Christ as your personal Lord and Savior. Number two involves following the Lord's command and statues, including the cheerful giving of your tithes and offerings.

God's promise to the believer who has made this preparation is that He will give them a Comforter (Parakletos) to assist them in completing His plan for their lives (John 14:16).

A key to understanding how God manifests His blessings in our lives is to appreciate that our act of worship in the cheerful giving of our tithes and offerings releases the divine protection of God, through His Holy Spirit, over our thoughts, plans, and actions. The Holy Spirit became an active agent, your personal advocate, in fulfilling God's promise spoken through the prophet Malachi when He said, "And I will rebuke the devourer [insects and plagues] for your sakes and he shall not destroy the fruits of your ground (Mal 3:11, AMP).

Our act of worship in the cheerful giving of our tithes and offerings releases the divine protection of God

---

Here is the problem with those of us who have robbed God of His tithes and offerings: "Ye are cursed with a curse" (Mal 3:9). How does the curse manifest itself? God revealed it to Moses when He declared the curses that would come upon His children who failed to hearken unto the voice of the Lord to carry out all His commandments and statutes (Deut 28:15). Moses declared, "Thou shall carry much seed out into the field, and shalt gather but little in; for the locust shall consume it" (Deut 28:38).

I believe the seed referred to by Moses is representative of our thoughts, planted by the Holy Spirit, that are continuously being devoured because of our disobedience to the commands and ordinances of the Lord. Because the locust (devourer) has consumed the "seeds of thought" planted by the Lord, so many Christians are living lives

50

that reflect only a small fraction of the fruit that God ordained for them to produce.

I want you to reflect for a minute on some of your lingering thoughts to do good (godly) things that you somehow can't seem to get around to doing. For some of you, it may be starting a business, going to college, building a home, starting a family, starting a school or a day care center, becoming a pastor, volunteering at your church or local community center, or tithing. For others it may be singing in the choir, volunteering at the soup kitchen, contributing to a welfare fund, organizing and participating in hospital visits or visits to the elderly, starting a mission to assist the poor, or something else.

Truth be told, some of you have had to think hard because these thoughts are dead and buried. They have been removed from your mind because you see them as impossible to achieve. They are thoughts consumed by the devourer. Yet each of those lingering thoughts that passes the tests is a seed planted by God. How do I know? Every good thing and every perfect gift is from above ... coming down from the Father of lights ... (James 1:17, NIV). Each of those thoughts, individually and collectively, reflects the plan of God for your life. A plan that has embedded in it the resources you need to successfully accomplish it to the honor and glory of God the Father.

For each of us, the devourer has manifested himself in many different forms: a busy lifestyle that doesn't allow time to think about or pursue your real dreams and aspirations; mental illness such as depression; a physical disease that strikes at the root of your plans; a spouse who discourages you from pursuing your dreams; a child whose actions stand up like a mountain before your path; lack of financial discipline or self-control that stands in the way; pride in all of its manifestations; fear that simply paralyzes you; and the list goes on.

The question each of us must ask ourselves is, am I robbing God? Each of us, through self-examination, must ask ourselves if we have gone away from responding positively to the Holy Spirit's administration of God's ordinances and commands within us and, as a result, allowed the devourer to strike at the root of God's plan for our lives. God's promise to those who bring all their tithes and offerings into His house is that He "will prevent pests from devouring your crops …" (Mal 3:11, NIV). God will protect the seed planted so that it may birth into action at the appointed time. Just as God protected the promise given to David that he would be crowned king over the children of Israel (1 Sam 16:1, 13), so too will He protect your thoughts, dreams, and aspirations, that they may be manifested into action to the glory and honor of God the Father.

While I was living in New York in the 1980s, the Lord laid on my heart the desire to formulate plans for starting a financial services company in the British Virgin Islands. At the time, I prepared a business plan. However, despite my efforts, nothing came of it. For years, the plan sat with no movement in sight. It was a seed planted in the earth. It was not until June 2003, more than fifteen years after the plans were completed, that God birthed the seed He had planted in my heart. Today our firm has partnered with Merrill Lynch and is fulfilling the plan of God to His honor and glory. God will do the same for you—the ball is in your court.

Attacks on the Fruit

Unlike the seed that is hidden and cannot be seen, the fruit is visible and is subject to a different set of attacks by the devourer. In our lives, the fruit represents the physical manifestation of our plans through actions that collectively lead to the fulfillment of God's plans for our lives.

Each of us must accept the reality that we will be attacked because of the manifestation of God's plan for our lives. Jesus declared that the thief comes but to steal, kill, and destroy (John 10:10). None of us is exempt from the work of the devourer. The adversary will do all in his power to make sure we do not complete God's plan for our lives. However, God's promise to those who obey and bring their tithes into the storehouse is that "your vine shall not cast her fruit before the time ..." (Mal 3:11).

The attacks of the devourer as a result of the manifestations of God's plan are many and varied. The Amplified Bible puts in brackets its elaboration of the devourer to include insects and plagues (Mal 3:11). Note the plural use of the words and reflect for a minute on the many different types of insects and plagues there are in the world, some of which are yet unknown. I believe that these represent the many different forms of attack the devourer will use against each of us in our pursuit of the plan God has ordained for us. They include all the attacks against your "seeds of thought" and more.

Remember, the devourer has been around from the foundation of the earth and has built up quite an array of strategies and weapons for his warfare against the plan of God. My encouragement to you is to remember the battle belongs to the Lord. As, the songwriter reminds us, "Jesus is stronger than Satan and sin; Satan to Jesus must bow" (Methodist Hymn Book, hymn 374, verse 3). If you are in the middle of an attack as you read this book, call on the name of Jesus and submit in your heart to the commands and ordinances of God. Then watch Him come to your defense in accordance with His promise: "The pests shall not devour your crops ..." (Mal 3:11, AMP).

An observation impressed upon me by the Holy Spirit as I reflected on the strategies and attacks of the devourer is that when the attack is external, it is often rooted in jealousy, covetousnesss, and insecurity. Satan will plant these seeds in someone and point them in your direction to unleash his attacks on you.

In 1 Samuel 17 and 18, we see the physical manifestation of God's plans for David's life being revealed before all of Israel. He fought and prevailed over Goliath and led Israel's army to victory in all his battles. In response, the "women came out of all the cities of Israel, singing and dancing, to meet King Saul, with (timbrels), with joy, and with instruments of music ... and said Saul had slain his thousands, and David his ten thousands" (1 Sam 18:6–7). The Bible tells us that Saul was angry because the saying displeased him, and his jealousy toward David was stirred up from that day forward (1 Sam 18:8–9, AMP). The seed of jealousy was planted in Saul by the devourer, and his sole obsession from that point on was to kill David—to destroy the fruit from the vine.

The manifestation of the spirit of jealousy in Saul toward David brings with it lessons that are critical for each of us to learn and apply as we travel along the road to fulfilling the plan of God in our lives:

- Affiliate yourself with individuals who are spiritually connected to the Lord.
- Beware of those connected to the devourer.
- Behave wisely.

Affiliate Yourself with Individuals Who Are Spiritually Connected to the Lord

In 1 Samuel 18:1, we learn the following: "When he [David] had made an end to speaking unto Saul, that the soul of Jonathan was knit with the soul of David, and Jonathan loved him as his own soul." Let me set the scene for you. David had just accomplished what no one in Saul's army was even willing to attempt—fighting against Goliath. He had not only fought him and won, but made way for the slaughter of the Philistine army. After being informed of all that David had done, Saul asked David, "Whose son art thou, thou young man?" (1 Sam 17:58). When David was finished revealing to Saul that which was hidden until now, jealousy sprang up in Saul, but love sprang forth in Jonathan's heart. From that time forth, Jonathan became an instrument God would use to preserve his plan for David's life.

We repeatedly see Jonathan risking his own life to save David from the wrath of Saul. On one occasion, after Saul gives a command to kill David, we see Jonathan's love for David rising above his loyalty to his father, as he says, "Saul, my father is seeking to kill you. Now therefore, take heed to yourself in the morning, and stay in a secret place and hide yourself" (1 Sam 19:2, AMP). While there is no specific reference to Jonathan's spiritual connection with God, there is ample evidence of it. The fruit of the Spirit—love, joy, peace, long-suffering, gentleness, goodness, faith, meekness, and temperance—springs forth from the pages of the

Bible and declares Jonathan's connection to God. Indeed, Jonathan's interactions with his father, his love and kindness toward David, and God's guidance and protection in war give ample testimony of his relationship with God.

Jonathan's connection to God and his love for David were not by chance. It was a part of God's master plan for David to fulfill His divine purpose. As God's plan for your life translates into actions, I strongly encourage you to remain consciously alert for those individuals whom God has ordained to be spiritual and physical protectors against the devourer. How will you know them? You will know them by their fruit. What fruit? The same fruit of the Spirit so easily found in Jonathan's life as well as the inexplicable love they have for you.

Remain consciously alert for those individuals whom God has ordained to be spiritual and physical protectors against the devourer

---

I give God thanks often for truly blessing me with my equivalents of Jonathan. They are mighty women of God who collectively remain to this day a tower of strength and a source of tremendous blessing to my entire family and me. Their prayers, unconditional love, godly wisdom, and guidance are the wind beneath my wings.

Beware of Those Connected to the Devourer

In stark contrast to Jonathan, Saul exhibited works of the flesh, including envy, jealousy, and hatred toward David. Have you ever told someone about a success you have had, or has someone found out about a promotion you received, and suddenly you feel a change in the way that person relates to you? The individual becomes cold and distant. A word of warning: beware of such individuals, for the evidence of the devourer is manifested. Do not keep company with them.

The Bible tells us that as David played his harp for Saul, there was a javelin in the king's hand, and he cast the javelin at David, saying, "I will smite David even to the wall with it" (1 Sam 18:10–11). Saul, in contrast to Jonathan had become an instrument of the devil's mandate to kill, steal, and destroy.

The saying "Sticks and stones can break my bones, but words can never hurt me" couldn't be further from the truth. Words often do more harm than sticks and stones could ever do. Oftentimes, the javelin the enemy throws at us involves words, the impact of which can only be avoided by the standard God lifts up by the truth of His word in our defense.

After Saul's attempt on David's life, the Bible tells us, "David escaped from his presence ..." My advice to you is that when you come in contact with the Saul spirit of envy and jealousy, follow David's example and remove yourself from its presence. The words that will be thrown at you may kill God's plan for your life.

---

when you come in contact with the Saul spirit of envy and jealousy, follow David's example and remove yourself from its presence

---

When Saul could not destroy David with his own hands, he sought to set him up so that the enemy of Israel could do the job:

And Saul said to David, Behold my elder daughter Merab, her will I give to thee to wife: only be thou valiant for me, and fight the Lord's battles. For Saul said, Let not mine hand be upon him, but let the hand of the Philistines be upon him (1 Sam 18:17).

What Saul had not fully considered was that all that he was plotting to do was part of God's master plan for David's life, and He had already provided divine protection and favor as part of that plan. No harm would come to David, for he was within the perfect will of God for his life. What Saul meant for evil, as he sent David into battle after battle, God used for David's good. In fact, 1 Samuel 18:16, tells us, "All of Israel and Judah loved David because he went out and came in before them."

When we, like David, find ourselves under the command or authority of someone we know is being influenced by the devourer to do us harm physically or spiritually, be encouraged by the guidance the Lord has provided for us through the inspired actions of David:

Behave Wisely

In the midst of Saul's attempts to destroy the manifest fruit of David's vine, the Bible tells us in 1 Samuel 18:14 that "David behaved himself wisely in all his ways; and the Lord was with him." Therein lies a critical lesson for each of us when we find ourselves under attack by the devourer: behave wisely in all your ways.

David was no stranger to attacks. Indeed, his past experiences had prepared him well for this chapter in his life. Out of his victories over the lion and the bear, he had come away with an invaluable lesson: "the battle is the Lord's" (1 Sam 17:47). David realized that his victory in each of those encounters was only possible through the divine assistance of the Lord. He understood that it was humanly impossible for him to defeat the lion and the bear by himself. Just as there had been another in the fiery furnace with Shadrach, Mesach, and Abendigo, there was another in the fight with him, and He was stronger than both the lion and bear combined. It was the Lord.

David further realized that his role was to behave wisely by living his life in accordance with the commands, statutes, and ordinances of the Lord. The benefit of this behavior was the presence of the Lord with him. God would be with him in every battle great or small. I believe that David concluded at the end of his quiet contemplation, If God be for me, who can be against me? (Rom 8:31).

The lessons learnt by David prepared him well for his encounter with Saul. In the midst of Saul's continued attempts on David's life, we see him acting and behaving according to the word of God at the prompting of the Holy Spirit. It would be natural for any person under attack to retaliate with like action, yet we do not see David rendering evil for Saul's evil. In 1 Samuel 26, an account is given of David's opportunity to kill the man who had become his enemy continually (1 Sam 18:29). Yet we see David acting on the instructions of the Lord not to stretch forth his hand against the Lord's anointed (1 Sam 26:11). Instead of rendering evil for evil, David went about doing good in opposition to the wishes of his own army. David's behavior prompted Jonathan to proclaim to his father Saul, "Let not the king sin against his servant David, for he has not sinned against you, and his deeds have been of good service to you" (1 Sam 19:4, AMP).

Not only did David do good by his actions, but indeed nowhere do we see David speaking evil of Saul or his lips speaking guilefully.

Instead, we see David seeking peace and pursuing it through Jonathan and by his words and actions. By behaving wisely in all his ways, David availed himself of *all* God's divine protection and defenses against his enemy. The word of God assures us, "The eyes of the Lord are over the righteous and His ears are open unto their prayers. Who is he that will harm you, if you be followers of that which is good?" (1 Pet 3:13).

What is important to observe as you reflect on David's response and actions in the face of Saul's continued attacks on his life is that they were directed by the prompting of the Holy Spirit. David himself reminds us, "The steps of a good man are ordered by the Lord" (Ps 37:23).

God's instructions for David's encounter with Saul, God's anointed, was indeed different from His instructions concerning Goliath, the uncircumcised Philistine and one who defied the armies of the Living God (1 Sam 17:26). In the case of Saul, God's instructions were ones of disengagement, while in the case of Goliath, God gave David the courage and strength of character to engage in one-on-one combat with a giant that all of Israel thought was unbeatable. In each case, though the strategy was different, David was victorious.

You too must seek out God's direction and guidance through prayer and fasting in every encounter with the devourer. His instructions for how you are to behave in each circumstance will be different. In some cases, His instruction will be one of disengagement, while in others it will be to engage the enemy. Remember, however, that you wrestle not against flesh and blood but against principalities, against powers, against the rulers of darkness of this world, against spiritual wickedness in high places (Eph 6:12). As a result, your engagement will always be spiritual first and often result in minimizing or eliminating any need for physical engagement. Think about it for a second. How do you defeat anger, fear, jealousy, envy, malice, covetousness, or hatred? These spiritual enemies can only be defeated through spiritual warfare.

Paul reminds us that the weapons of our warfare are not physical (weapons of flesh and blood) but are mighty before God for the overthrow and destruction of strongholds (2 Cor 10:4, AMP). Those weapons include prayer, fasting, praise and worship. What I love about the Lord's designation of the Christians' weapons is that you do not need to be rich, famous, well connected, have the right address, educated, attend the right church, or have the right last name to access them. All God's children have equal access. If we apply the weapons of our warfare with the guidance and assistance of the Holy Spirit in each encounter, we will discover what David did. Victory is assured every time.

The benefits to those of us who behave wisely in the face of attacks by the devourer are real and practical in our pursuit of fulfilling God's plan for our lives: God will grant favor, and His presence will be with us.

God Will Grant Favor

Repeatedly, as we read the story of David's encounters with Saul, we see the Lord granting favor to him as he behaved wisely. In 1 Samuel, we read, "David went out whithersoever Saul sent him, and behaved himself wisely: and Saul set him over the men of war, and he was accepted in the sight of all the people and also in the sight of Saul's servants" (1 Sam 18:5). We further learned that Jonathan (heir to the throne of King Saul) "stripped himself of the robe that was upon him, and gave it to David, and his garments, even to his sword, and to his bow, and to his girdle" (1 Sam 18:4). That is favor.

Psalm 84 declares, "The Lord is a sun and shield; the Lord bestows favor and honor; no good thing will He withhold from them whose walk is blameless" (Ps 84:11, NIV). This passage reveals that the Lord himself was the source of David's favor. Indeed, God is the source of all favor. What He did for David, God will do for all His children as they walk along the pathway to fulfilling His plan for their lives. The truth is, God has been granting each of us favor before we ever came to know Him or accept Him as our personal Lord and Savior.

When I was attending The BVI High School, our volleyball team was invited to St. Croix to play in a tournament. While in St. Croix, one of the students asked if I would like to use his car to drive, and I readily and enthusiastically said yes. The only problem was that I was only about twelve at the time and did not have a driver's license. However, that important fact did not stop me from accepting the offer.

After the game, my friends and I got into the car and headed for the apartment we were staying in. On the way, we got a brilliant idea to explore what it feels like driving on a highway. With all the enthusiasm of a twelve-year-old, I headed up the highway as fast as the car would go, with my brother Keith and friends laughing and having a good time. When we got a certain distance along the highway, we decided to turn around and head back home. There was only one problem: it had begun to rain.

Full of inexperience, I ignored the fact that it was now raining and headed back with the same level of enthusiasm. As we came to a corner, my inexperience manifested itself in the worst possible way. Instead of slowing down around the corner, I kept the same speed, and the car spun out of control. For what seemed like an eternity, the car twisted and turned on the slippery road. Suddenly, the car came to a sudden stop in a rough patch of scrub on the side of the road. After it stopped, I remember looking across the road and seeing a man dressed in white. However, when I looked again, he was gone.

Minutes later, a truck came by, and the driver asked if we were hurt and offered assistance. We were never so happy to see somebody in our lives. The driver informed us of how blessed we were. He explained that had we gone just a little further, we would have gone over a deep embankment, which would have meant sure injury or even death to some or all of us.

I remember going back to the apartment, trembling with the burden of knowing that I could have been responsible for the death of four young men. I did not sleep that night. I kept replaying the accident in my mind and remembering that man on the side of the street. When I asked the others if they had seen him, all said they had not. After a while, I forgot about him as the accident faded from memory.

Many years later, close to the time that I accepted Jesus Christ as my personal Lord and Savior, I stayed at home alone one Sunday morning because I didn't feel well. Later on in the morning, I got up, went downstairs, and turned on the television to Trinity Broadcasting Network (TBN). The late Bishop G. E. Patterson was preaching a sermon titled "If God Be for You, Who Can Be against You." As I listened, the Holy Spirit took me back to the accident on the side of the road and showed me the man dressed in white again. He said these words to me: **"It was Me you saw on the side of the road.**

I was there to protect you and preserve you to preach the word of God as I have told you." I cried and cried that Sunday morning and gave God thanks for His grace and mercy that had kept me. Even before I had accepted him, God had granted me favor and had preserved my life from the devourer so that I could complete His plan for my life to his honor and glory.

My story is not unique. Repeatedly, as I speak to my brothers and sisters in Christ, I hear countless stories of God's favor being poured out among His Children as they pursue the plan of God for their lives. His helping hand in time of trouble, sickness, or battle is available to you today free of charge as long as you accept Jesus Christ as your personal Lord and Savior and behave wisely by following His commands and statues. Proverbs reminds us of the following: "For he who finds me (Jesus) finds life and obtains favor from the LORD" (Prov 8:35, NAS).

God's Presence Will Be with You

The benefits of behaving wisely extend beyond favor to include the very presence of God being with you. In 1 Samuel, "David behaved himself wisely in all his ways; and the Lord was with him" (1 Sam 18:14). Indeed, the Bible goes on to indicate, "when Saul saw that he (David) behaved himself very wisely, he was afraid of him" (1 Sam 18:15). Like Paul, David could declare, "If God be for us, who can be against us?" (Rom 8:31). God's presence is still with His children today, actively engaged in helping us achieve the plan of God for our lives.

One of my sisters in Christ tells the story of her being prompted by the Holy Ghost to get up during the night to pray for one of her sons.

She obeyed the prompting and found herself praying fervently for her son. What she had not realized at the time was that at that very hour, her son had been carjacked and placed in the trunk of the car, left to die. Her son reported that he had tried to get the trunk open repeatedly but just couldn't do it. Suddenly, he felt the presence of God in the trunk with him, and it became clear what he must do to get the trunk opened. Within minutes, the trunk flew open, and he emerged alive and well.

Because of God's response to a mother's prayers, her son was able to defeat the adversary's attempt to destroy the plan of God for his life. God's presence made the difference between life and death. His presence will make the difference in battle for you as you behave wisely in the pursuit of God's plan for your life.

I am still learning to behave wisely in the face of attacks by the adversary. I am the first to admit that it is not easy. So often when you do, others see it as weakness and foolishness. In those times, I am comforted by the word of God, which reminds us that "the foolishness of God is wiser than men; and the weakness of God is stronger than men (1 Cor 1:25). I am further comforted by my own personal experience of witnessing God fulfill His promise of favor, protection, and deliverance as I behave wisely in His sight. Over the years, I have fully come to believe that we serve a faithful God—one who is 100 percent committed to our successful completion of His plan for our lives. I encourage you to follow the examples He has provided to us through the life of David, remembering always that the battle is not yours. It's the Lord's.

7

Wait on the Lord

—Psalm 27:14

In a world where having it now is the measure for being blessed, we all run the risk of saying harsh things against God when His promises do not appear to manifest according to our timing. God reminded the children of Israel of their harsh sayings against Him, when they said, "It is futile to serve God. What did we gain by carrying out His requirements?" (Mal 3:14, NIV).

As children of God, we must guard our thoughts, words, and actions from thinking, speaking, and acting foolishly before God. I remind you of the following:

> *God is not a man, that He should lie, nor a son of man, that He should repent; has He said, and will He not do it? Or hath He spoken, and will He not make it good?* (Num 23:19, NAS).

If God said to bring all the tithes into the storehouse, and that He would pour out a blessing, for which there would not be room enough to receive it, I believe it unconditionally. Our attitude should be to let God be true and every man be a liar (Rom 3:4). If He said it; I believe it; I apply it; I receive it. Amen. Does it mean I receive it right away? No! God has planted a seed, and you must now apply your faith and believe that it will produce a rich harvest in your life according to the will of God in due season.

If we received it all at once, we would make a mess of it physically and spiritually. Instead, as the seed germinates slowly and the plant goes on with its business of producing its fruit according to its predetermined season, so too does God release his financial blessings in our lives a little at a time, while at the same time preparing us for the harvest according to the work we have been assigned to complete.

Will it be the same progression or the same season for everyone? No! The same way different plants mature and bear their fruits at different seasons, so too will we produce our fruits and reap our blessings at different times. No two plans are alike.

That's where we often falter. We look at other people and become jealous of what God is doing in their lives, not recognizing that our season will come according to the plan and purpose of God for our lives. Worse yet, we look at those who appear to be prospering outside of the will of God and call them blessed. We conclude this in our hearts: "Evildoers prosper, and even those who challenge God escape" (Mal 3:15, NIV). The result is that we abort the plan of God for our lives and go our own way, thereby forfeiting God's best for us. I want to encourage you today to stick to the plan and wait on the Lord.

In 1 Kings 18:41, we see Elijah speaking a word of faith to Ahab, saying, "Get thee up, eat and drink; for there is a sound of abundance of rain." Elijah's declaration of truth was grounded in the word of the Lord that came to him, saying, "I will send rain upon the earth" in response to the sore famine in Samaria (1 Ki 18:2–3). In anticipation of the fulfillment of God's promise, the Bible records the following:

> *And Elijah went up to the top of Carmel; and he cast himself down upon the earth, and put his face between his knees,*
>
> *And said to his servant, Go up now, look toward the sea. And he went up, and looked, and said, There is nothing. And he said, Go again seven times.*
>
> *And it came to pass at the seventh time, that he said, Behold, there ariseth a little cloud out of the sea like a man's hand. And he said, Go up, and say to Ahab, Prepare thy chariot, and get thee down, that the rain stop thee not.*
>
> *And it came to pass in the mean while, that the heaven was black with clouds and wind, and there was a great rain ...* (1 Ki 18:42–45).

Can you imagine how Elijah felt? He had heard from God that it was going to rain after three years of famine in the land. He had acted out his faith in the face of grave danger by personally informing the king, who blamed him exclusively for the famine in the land. Lastly, he had placed himself in a position of worship and complete reliance on God to fulfill His promise. Yet every time he sent his servant to check on the manifestation of the promised rain, the response was, "There is nothing." There was nothing the first six times.

Elijah had every reason to give up and go in a different direction. Indeed, in the flesh, Elijah had every reason to say it was futile to serve God and move away from the plan that God had ordained for him to follow. Instead, Elijah stayed in a position of worship and complete trust in Almighty God and waited expectantly on the Lord.

Psalm 27:14 reminds us that we ought to "wait on the Lord: be of good courage, and He shall strengthen thine heart: wait, I say, on the Lord."

The construction of this verse of scripture speaks volume of the tone and urgency of what the Lord wanted to have communicated to the reader. Upon a careful reading of the verse, you can almost hear David shouting, "Wait on the Lord!" The tone reflects one that is directed to someone who is about to do something outside the will of God, and a deliberate attempt is being made to get his attention.

I believe that as Elijah received the reports from his servant, the full weight and substance of what David was communicating in Psalm 27:14 resonated with him, and he determined in his mind that no matter how negative the report, he was going to stick to the plan and "wait on the Lord."

Elijah's actions reflect a man who had heard from God and had received in faith all that he was told. He believed without wavering that God was able to do what He had promised: "send rain upon the earth." That faith was grounded in a history of God performing miracles in Elijah's life. You and I must follow Elijah's example, knowing that God is the Lord of all flesh, and that there is nothing too hard for Him to do (Jer 32:27).

The truth is that it is never easy to wait. Yet repeatedly God encourages us in scripture to do just that. I believe the stern reminder in Psalm 27:14 is designed to cause us to reflect on the sovereignty of God over everything that concerns us. Remember, He is the chief architect of the plan for our lives. He knows the intricate details. He has left nothing out. Everything is in place, and He is continually communicating the details of your plan to the Holy Spirit, who is the master builder of what God has designed.

Holy Spirit... is the master builder of what God has designed

---

The stage has been set before the foundation of the world. Your resources are in place, your workers are in place, your consolers are in place, your finances are in place, your adversaries are in place, your prayer warriors are in place, the weapons of your warfare are in place, and your spiritual gifts are in place. Whatever you need to accomplish what God has planned for your life is already in place.

Like the patriarchs of old, along your journey to fulfilling God's plan for your life, you will have to continually wait on the Lord to guide you. As scripture reminds, "the steps of a good man are ordered by the Lord" (Ps 37:23). Remember that He is omnipresent. Everything is always before Him, and nothing is hidden from Him. He is in a unique position to lead you in the way that you should go.

As we wait, God's promise is that He "shall strengthen your heart" (Ps 27:14). I believe that strength comes to each of us as we worship God during our time of waiting. Remember that genuine worship— the kind that springs out of a personal relationship with God, the kind that lets go and lets God, the kind that say it's all about Jesus, the kind that says we are totally dependent on Jesus —brings us into the presence of the Lord. The psalmist David reminds us that in the presence of the Lord, there is "fullness of joy: at His right hand, there are pleasures evermore" (Ps 16:11). Scripture further reminds us that the joy of the Lord is our strength (Neh 8:10).

Think about this. As you worship the Lord, He fills you up with joy that becomes your strength. The dictionary defines joy as the expectation of something good. If we take this definition and replace the word joy in the passage of scripture from Nehemiah, the passage of scripture would read, "The expectation of something good from the Lord is our strength." As you wait on the Lord, I encourage you to get up and worship Him in spirit and in truth. I believe that He will reveal to you what is about happen and replace your doubt, your sorrow, your disappointment, and your pain with the expectation of something good from Him, which will give you the strength you need to wait for Him as He brings about that which He has promised.

As you worship the Lord, He fills you up with
joy that becomes your strength

In Acts 16, we read about the story of Paul and Silas's imprisonment in Macedonia after they were beaten. As they sat in prison and waited for what would come next, it is important to observe that nothing happened until they decided to worship God. The passage revealed that it was not until about midnight that Paul and Silas began their period of worship, first with prayers and then with praise. I believe that as they set their hearts to worship God and began to pray, the Holy Ghost gave them a revelation of what was about to happen, and they were filled with joy and strengthened. Immediately, Paul and Silas got up and began praising the Lord with loud voices. When the praises go up, deliverance comes down. That is exactly what happened. As Acts 16:26 tells us, "Suddenly there was a great earthquake, so that the foundations of the prison were shaken; and immediately all the doors were opened, and everyone's bands were loosed."

I want to encourage you today to stay in your position of worship. God is about to reveal some things to you that will fill you up with joy and give you the strength to carry on. That is exactly what happened to Elijah.

In spite of the negative reports from his servant, Elijah stayed in a position of worship before almighty God. On the seventh try, God revealed what was about to happen by giving him a sign of a distant cloud about the size of a man's hand. It may not have seemed like much to the natural eye, but to Elijah it was a sign from God himself that He was about to do that which He had promised. We are told that Elijah immediately gave instructions to his servant to "Go up and say unto Ahab, Prepare thy chariot, and get thee down that the rain stop thee not" (1 Ki 18:44).

You can almost feel the energy and confidence in Elijah's words: *Go* and *Prepare*. I believe it is no accident that these words are capitalized. They draw attention to the countenance of Elijah, which was one of renewed strength and faith in the promise of God as he gave the command to his servant. His patience was about to be rewarded.

We are told that after Elijah got up from his position of worship, "the heaven was black with clouds and wind, and there was a great rain … And the hand of the Lord was on Elijah; and he girded up his loins, and ran before Ahab to the entrance of Jezreel" (1 Ki 18:45–46). I want you to reflect on what was happening for a minute. Ahab, the king, had gotten into his chariot that was being drawn by the finest horses in all Israel and was headed down the hill, galloping at full speed as the clouds formed in the heavens. As the heavens became black with clouds and the wind blew, Elijah took off on foot, ran past Ahab and his chariot, and waited for him at the entrance of Jezreel. That is truly amazing but not impossible. Jesus himself reminded us that what is impossible with man is possible with God (Luke 18:27).

As I reflected on this incredible story, the Lord reminded me of the passage of scripture from Isaiah 40:31:

> *But they that wait upon the Lord shall renew their strength; they shall mount up with wings as eagles; they shall run and not be weary; they shall walk and not faint.*

The Holy Spirit impressed upon me that because Elijah waited on Him, this scripture came alive in his life. The hand of the Lord mounted up Elijah with wings like eagles and gave him the speed of an eagle soaring high above the earth to run past Ahab's chariot to the entrance of Jezreel.

I hope this revelation encourages you and fills you with joy as you wait for the fulfillment of God's promise in your life. Too many of God's children have moved away from the plan of God for their lives because they believe that their wait would be in vain. Some have looked at others moving ahead and believed that they would never catch up if they don't act now. That is where Saul was when he found himself in a position of an advancing superior Philistine army without receiving a word from God through His prophet Samuel. Instead of waiting on the Lord, Saul took matters into his own hands and forced himself to offer burnt offerings to the Lord, a task reserved for the priesthood.

That decision was the beginning of the downfall of Saul. Upon hearing Saul's reasoning for the decision, Samuel responded, saying,

> *Thou hast done foolishly: thou has not kept the commandment of the Lord thy God, which He commanded thee: for now the Lord would have established thy kingdom upon Israel for ever.*
>
> *But now thy kingdom shall not continue: the Lord hath sought Him a man after his own heart, and the Lord hath commanded him to be captain over his people, because thou has not kept that which the Lord has commanded thee* (1 Sam 13:13–14).

Wow! Because of Saul's decision not to wait on the Lord, he forfeited his position and standing with the Lord. No explanation, no matter how credible it appears in the eyes of man, was good enough. God's requirement for the leader of His people was that he should reverently "fear the LORD, and serve him, and obey His voice …" (1 Sam 12:14) Saul failed the test by not waiting on the Lord. As the army advanced, Saul failed to ground his faith in the words spoken by the Lord through his prophet Samuel, saying, "For the LORD will not forsake his people for his great name's sake …" (1 Sam 12:22). No matter how strong the Philistine army appeared to be, Saul served a God who was stronger.

I encourage you again to "wait on the Lord." Elijah's story reminds us that no matter how long God has required you to wait, He is able to propel you into your destiny by the power of His mighty hand. Wait on Him today and be strengthened as He sets the stage for your next move along the pathway of fulfilling His plan for your life.

8

"I have finished the work which thou gavest Me to do."

—John 17:4

In the gospel of John, Jesus gives us a perfect picture of what fulfillment looks and feels like when He prayed, "I have glorified thee on the earth: I have finished the work which thou gavest me to do" (John 17:4). The ideal for each of us after we have lived out our lives on this earth is to stand before Jesus on that day and be able to repeat those words. Paul puts it this way at the end of his journey: "I have fought the good fight, I have finished my course, I have kept the faith. Henceforth there is laid up for me a crown of righteousness which the Lord, the righteous judge, shall give me at that day: and not me only, but unto all them that love His appearing" (2 Tim 4:7). The sincerity and humility with which these words are spoken by Paul reflect a deep sense of gratitude for the grace and mercies of God in assisting him to complete the plan of God for his life. Paul's parting message to each of us is that this same reward is available to all who avail themselves of God's grace and mercies in completing His plan for their lives. Our job is to finish the work God gave us to do or, as Paul puts it, finish the course.

The challenge for each of us as children of God is to gain an understanding of the work God has preordained for us to do. As Paul reminds us in the book of Ephesians, "... we are His workmanship, created in Christ Jesus unto good works, which God hath before ordained that we should walk in them" (Eph 2:10). The Amplified Bible put it this way:

> *For we are God's (own) handiwork (His workmanship), recreated in Christ Jesus, (born anew) that we may do those good works which God predestined (planned beforehand) for us (taking paths which He prepared ahead of time), that we should walk in them (living the good life which He prearranged and made ready for us to live)* (Eph 2:10 AMP).

It is important to observe that the good works that God has given us to do are found in Christ Jesus. We should further observe that those good works have been prepared for each of us before the foundation of the world. God informed Jeremiah, "Before I formed thee in the belly I knew thee; and before thou camest forth out of the womb I sanctified thee, and I ordained thee a prophet unto the nations" (Jer 1:5). Before you were born, God had already ordained for you the work you are to accomplish in His name.

I believe that after you have accepted Jesus Christ as your personal Lord and Savior, the Holy Spirit will reveal to you the work that you have been assigned to accomplish in Christ Jesus and manifest in you the spiritual gifts necessary for the successful completion of your work. As Paul reminds us in Ephesians, "But unto every one of us is given grace [God's unmerited favor] according to the measure of the gift of Christ … And he gave some, apostles; and some, prophets; and some, evangelists; and some, pastors and teachers" (Eph 4:7–11). Whatever your assignment is from God, it will always include some element of telling others about Jesus Christ. I believe that if this element is missing, you have not yet received your complete assignment from the Holy Ghost. Remember, the Holy Spirit is accomplishing the work through you, and His primary job is to glorify Jesus (John 16:14).

In accomplishing the work that is given to each of us, Paul further reminds us:

> *The manifestation of the Spirit is given to every man … for one is given by the Spirit the word of wisdom; to another the word of knowledge by the same Spirit; to another faith by the same Spirit; to another the gifts of healing by the same Spirit; to another the working of miracles; to another prophecy; to another discerning of spirits; to another divers kinds of tongues; to another the interpretations of tongues. But all these worketh that one and the selfsame Spirit, dividing to every man severally as he will* (1 Cor 12:7–11).

The manifestation of the gifts of the Spirit in every believer makes his work effective. Those gifts will manifest according to the work you have been given to do, and they will manifest according to the timing and plan of God for your life.

The manifestation of the gifts of the Spirit in every believer makes his work effective

---

I can recall two women praying over me, trying to evoke the gift of speaking in tongues in my life. The more they prayed, the more I felt nothing. After some time, they gave up, and I felt really tired and drained. It was a useless exercise, one that I have vowed will not happen again. Why? The word of God tells us it is the Holy Spirit that assigns our spiritual gifts (1 Cor 12:11). I am therefore confident that whatever spiritual gifts have been given to me will manifest in time for me to accomplish my work to the glory of God the Father. The same applies to you.

The successful accomplishment of those good works built on the foundation of Christ Jesus will bring glory to His name. Paul reminds us in 1 Corinthians, "For no man can lay a foundation other than the one which is laid, which is Jesus Christ." (1 Cor 3:11, NAS). On that day, it is the sum of those good works done in partnership with God that Christ will reward with the greeting "Well done, good and faithful servant … Enter thou into the joy of thy Lord" (Mat 25:23).

I want to encourage you that wherever you are in life, it is not too late to receive your assignment from God to complete the work assigned to you in Christ Jesus. Abraham was seventy-five and Moses was eighty when God revealed to them their paths. Don't let age discourage you. As Paul observed, "Christ Jesus came into the world to save sinners: of whom I am chief" (1 Tim 1:15). Don't let your past, no matter how sinful, be an obstacle. God's grace is sufficient for you. Go run your race and finish the work God has given you to do with the confidence that "if God be for you, who can be against you?" (Rom 8:31).

I can vividly recall the night that the Holy Spirit showed me the work God had preordained for me to accomplish on His behalf. I had accepted Jesus Christ as my personal Lord and Savior only a short time before. One night, about five months later, as I was lying on my bed, I heard an audible voice calling my name: **"Meade … Meade."** I answered, "Yes, Lord." He said, **"You have not done what I asked you to do."** I asked, "What, Lord?" He responded, **"Pentecost has come and gone, and my people still don't understand the power there is in the Holy Ghost."** I questioned, "What must I do, Lord?" He said, **"Preach."**

What has been truly wonderful about God's revelation of His plan for my life is my sense of place and purpose. I feel confident that if I remain faithful and obedient in following His plan, He will provide me with all the spiritual gifts that I need to be effective in accomplishing the work he has given me to do. His Holy Spirit will guide me in the things I ought to say and do and will deliver me in the time of trouble. I am further encouraged by Paul's testimony to Timothy during the period leading up to His departure: "The Lord shall deliver me from every evil work, and preserve me unto His heavenly Kingdom …" (2 Tim 4:18). He will do the same for each of us as we walk along the path to fulfilling His plan for each of our lives.

The Role of Our Financial Blessings

Along the path to fulfilling the work of God for my life, I have come to understand that the financial blessing we crave and seek is only a means to fulfilling the plan of God for our lives. When we apply the wealth that the Lord has given to us in accomplishing His plan for our lives, we bring glory to His name. Our reward on earth is joy, peace, and righteousness in the Holy Ghost. Our heavenly reward on that day is to hear these words from Jesus: "Well done, good and faithful servant … Enter thou into the joy of thy Lord" (Mat 25:23). That reward is priceless and far greater than any reward wealth can give.

When we apply the wealth that the Lord has given to us in accomplishing His plan for our lives, we bring glory to His name

---

I remember desiring to purchase furniture for our home and the Lord specifically lying on my heart that I should wait until His appointed time. When that time came, the Lord provided all the money needed to purchase the furniture in cash. As Sandra and I looked at the furniture we would eventually purchase, the Lord spoke to me and said that He was permitting us to purchase the furniture because we would entertain giants in the faith in our home. Not long after we had purchased the furniture, the Lord gave me a vision of Bishop T. D. Jakes sitting in our living room, being entertained on the furniture that we bought. Three months later, Bishop T. D. Jakes visited the British Virgin Islands to preach the word of God and sat in our living room in the exact place the Lord had revealed to me. What am I saying? The financial blessing I received to purchase the furniture was only a means to fulfilling the plan of God for my family to entertain giants of the faith in our home.

Bishop Jakes's work in the British Virgin Islands is still having a great spiritual impact today, and I cannot describe the great feeling of joy and satisfaction my family has experienced by advancing the plan of God for our lives.

David also recognized that the wealth he had accumulated was for God's plan. Toward the end of David's life, we see a man who had come to the full understanding that all that he had accomplished and all the wealth that He had accumulated were to fulfill the plan of God for his life. In recognition of this fact, David dedicated all the silver and gold that he received from all the nations he subdued for building God's house (2 Sam 8:11). David's reward for using his blessings to accomplish the plan of God for his life was fulfillment as reflected in the concluding statements regarding David's life: "And David the king also rejoiced with great joy" (1 Chr 29:9) and "he died in a good old age, full of days, riches, and honour ..." (1 Chr 29:28).

In 1 Chronicles 29:6–9, we also learn that the leaders of families, the officers of the tribes of Israel, the commanders of thousands and commanders of hundreds, and the officials in charge of the king's war gave willingly of their wealth toward the work of the house of the Lord. The passages revealed that the people rejoiced at the willing response of their leaders—for they had given willingly and with perfect hearts to the Lord: and David the king also rejoiced with great joy. Among the children of Israel, there was celebration, great joy, and happiness. Why? In an act of worship and reverence to the sovereignty of God over their lives, they had wholeheartedly applied their wealth to accomplishing the plan of God for their lives.

In contrast to David and the children of Israel's dedication of their wealth unto the Lord, we saw David's son Salomon apply his wealth in pursuit of worldly possessions and pleasures he believed would bring him happiness and fulfillment. However, upon reflection of his life, Solomon observed:

> *I made me great works; I builded me houses; I planted me vineyards: I made me gardens and orchards, and I planted trees in them of all kind of fruits: I made me pools of water, to water therewith the wood that bringeth forth trees: I got me servants and maidens,*

and had servants born in my house; also I had great possessions of great and small cattle above all that were in Jerusalem before me: I gathered me also silver and gold and the peculiar treasures of kings and of the provinces: I gat me men singers and women singers, and the delights of the sons of men, as musical instruments and that of all sorts ... I was great, and increased more than all that were before me in Jerusalem ... And whatsoever my eyes desired I kept not from them, I withheld not my heart from any joy ... [And he concluded] All was vanity and vexation of spirit, and there was no profit under the sun (Eccl 2:4–11).

Solomon, arguably the richest man who ever lived, pursued fulfillment through wine, great works, wealth, aesthetics pleasures, and fame. Yet all these failed to bring lasting satisfaction to the wisest man of all times (the King James Study Bible commentary, page 998). Solomon had pursued happiness with his financial blessings outside of the plan of God for his life, and the result was a king that sat on his throne with a frowning countenance dark with despair (Ellen White Commentary Deluxe Study Bible, King James Version, page 639). Today, more than three thousand years later, we see people, Christians included, attempting to find fulfillment in the pursuit of all that Solomon declared vanity and vexation of spirit, with the same result. In surveying the whole matter, Solomon concluded that our whole duty is to fear God and keep His commandments (Eccl 12:13).

I want to challenge each of you to follow these words of immeasurable wisdom: Our ultimate success in the sight of the Lord is only achieved in obeying His commands and statues.

Our ultimate success in the sight of the Lord is only achieved in obeying His commands and statues

When we apply the financial blessings that we have received through our obedience to accomplishing His work ordained for us as revealed by the Holy Spirit, God rewards us with His joy, peace, happiness on the earth and blesses us with the priceless gift of the words "Well done, good and faithful servant … Enter thou into thy joy of thy Lord" (Mat 25:23) as we enter His eternal kingdom."

9

Redeeming the time

Having reached this point in the book, some of you may be saying to yourselves, I am so far away from the plan of God for my life that there is no way I will even be able to unlock God's financial blessing. I want to assure you that before the foundation of the world, God knew that you would be reading this chapter of the book at this very minute. That same God, who has numbered every hair on your head, has marked out the details of the plan to restore all the years that the locust has eaten (Joel 2:25). No matter what your current financial situation may be, I want you to be encouraged that God has the power to redeem the time and restore you to the place He ordained for you before the foundation of the world.

In 2 Kings 4, an account is given of a certain woman whose husband had died and the creditors had come to take away her two sons to be bondsmen. Talk about a desperate situation. Yet in the midst of it, her actions allowed God to perform a mighty miracle that took her and her family from the brink of financial disaster to a place of financial abundance.

What I have come to love about the Lord is that He is not a respecter of persons (Acts 10:34). What He did for this widow, He will do for you. Her story revealed an important truth. The road to your financial success is already mapped out. It's up to you to follow the path and unlock the blessing that God has ordained for you.

This widow's actions and responses have within them the key that will unlock God's financial blessing for your life, no matter where you find yourself today. Read the passage of scripture below, taken from 2 Kings 4:1–7, and let's examine together the steps this widow took to achieve financial abundance.

> *Now there cried a certain woman of the wives of the sons of the prophets unto Elisha, saying, Thy servant my husband is dead; and thou knowest that thy servant did fear the Lord: and the creditor is come to take unto him my two sons to be bondmen.*
>
> *And Elisha said unto her, What shall I do for thee? Tell me, what hast thou in the house? And she said, Thine handmaid hath not any thing in the house, save a pot of oil.*
>
> *Then he said, Go, borrow thee vessels abroad of all thy neighbours, even empty vessels; borrow not a few.*
>
> *And when thou art come in, thou shalt shut the door upon thee and upon thy sons, and shalt pour out into all those vessels, and thou shalt set aside that which is full.*
>
> *So she went from him, and shut the door upon her and her sons, who brought the vessels to her, and she poured out.*

And it came to pass, when the vessels were full, that she said unto her son, Bring me yet a vessel. And he said unto her, There is not a vessel more. And the oil stayed.

Then she came and told the man of God. And he said, Go, sell the oil, and pay thy debt, and live thou and thy children of the rest.

Step 1. She looked to the man of God (Elisha) for help: So often when we find ourselves in financial difficulties, we look everywhere but to Jesus. We look to friends, family members, lending institutions, fortune-tellers, and the list goes on. This was not the case for this widow. The Bible tells us she cried unto the man of God (Elisha). I believe her cry was one full of confidence that the God with him was able to do something about her situation. Therein lies the revelation about the first key that unlocks the door. In the midst of your financial crisis, if you cry unto the Lord, confident that He is able to do something about it, God will respond and show himself mighty in your circumstance. In Psalm 18:6, 17, David declares, "In my distress I called upon the Lord and cried unto my God: He heard my voice out of His temple, and my cry came before Him, even unto His ears … He delivered me from my strong enemy and from them which hated me: for they were too strong for me."

The key is to cry out confidently to the Lord. That confidence comes out of a relationship with the Lord. What is your relationship with Jesus? The widow firmly established her relationship with Elisha when she informed him that his servant, her husband, was dead (2 Ki 4:1). I believe that it is not an accident that her husband is referred to as a servant. As a servant, her husband went about doing the things that his master Elisha instructed him to do. Put another way, he went about being obedient to the commands and instructions of his master. Elisha's response to this man's widow indicates that he was a good and faithful servant and therefore fully entitled to all the resulting benefits.

Again I ask, what is your relationship with Jesus? This relationship is established in accordance with Romans 10:9 (NIV), wherein Paul, a servant of Jesus, instructs, "If you confess with your mouth, "Jesus is Lord," and believe in your heart that God raised him from the dead, you will be saved. That confession with your mouth and belief in your heart will open up the way for God to respond to your situation according to His plan for your life.

Step 2. She acknowledged her husband's fear of the Lord: This fear was a reverent fear, one that acknowledged that the fear of the Lord is the beginning of knowledge (Prov 1:7). Her husband's fear, like Joshua's, committed him to a careful observance to do according to all the law that Elisha had commanded him, turning not from it to the right hand or to the left with the humble expectation that his way would be made prosperous. In acknowledging her husband's fear of the Lord, she was declaring to Elisha his eligibility to receive of the promises of God. As Psalm 34:9 reminds us, "There is no want to them that fear Him." Are you eligible to receive the promise of God? As you reflect on your past, many of you will answer no. Don't stay there; I bring you good news. If you commit in your heart now to reverently fear God and diligently follow His commands and statutes, He who sees and knows the future will bless you financially today, fully knowledgeable of every action you will take and every decision you will make in the future. You may be looking at your outward appearance, but God sees your heart (1 Sam 16:7). He knows that in Christ you have become a new creature, that old things are passed away and behold all things are become new (2 Cor 5:17). Just think—all your sins are instantly forgiven and cast in the sea of forgetfulness, separated from you as far as the east is from the west, thereby positioning you to receive God's blessings for your life. I encourage you to commit to a reverent fear of God today and let him manifest His divine plan for your life.

Step 3. She committed all she had to the Lord in faith: I want each of us to be encouraged by the fact that whatever our current situation is, the Lord is not surprised or caught off guard by it. Remember, each day of our lives was written down in His book before any of them came to be (Ps 139:16, NIV). His promise to each of us in the midst of our circumstance is that He will never leave us or forsake us. That promise is more secure than the ground on which we stand. His word declares that heaven and earth shall pass away, but his words will never pass away (Mat 24:35, NIV).

Take heart in this truth: Before the foundation of the world, He has made provision for a way of escape out of your financial difficulties. That way of escape may be through something physical or through something invisible, such as a talent. For the widow, it was a pot of oil sitting in her home. What is evident from the reading of the widow's story is that she was not aware that the pot of oil was her way of escape. It took Elisha's gift of discernment to reveal it to her. God whispered the details of His plan of escape concerning this widow to His prophet and instructed him to ask, What hast thou in the house? (2 Ki 4:2). Knowledgeable that "death and life are in the power of the tounge" her response, committed to God in faith, gave life and power to all the elements of the solution that God had provided as her way of escape (Prov 18:21). As you struggle through this period of financial difficulty, I want to encourage you to commit in faith that which God has revealed as your way of escape, thereby releasing God's power to unlock your financial blessing.

Before the foundation of the world, He has made provision for a way of escape out of your financial difficulties

---

I am reminded of the hidden five loaves and two fish that, once revealed, were committed unto the Lord in Matthew 14:16–20, to feed the multitude that was gathered to hear Jesus. It seemed impossible that so little could make a difference in feeding five thousand men, in addition to women and children. But after Jesus blessed it and broke it, there was enough to feed everyone, with twelve full baskets left over. Truly, little is much when God is in it.

What is in your home or business today that you are not even aware that God has given you as a means of escape from your current financial difficulties? I encourage you to seek the Lord in prayer for the answer. The answer may come through a man or woman of God. It may come to you in a vision or dream. It may come through inspiration by the Holy Spirit as you read the word or listen to a sermon. However it comes, acknowledge God's provision verbally and commit it unto the Lord in faith. Why verbally? As the scripture reminds us, "Death and life are in the power of the tongue" (Prov 18:21). A liberating force is released when a child of God speaks in faith. That force is stronger than any financial chain that has you bound today. Be encouraged that no one visible or invisible can stop that force from completing its task once it is released. Remember, "Jesus is stronger than Satan and sin; Satan to Jesus must bow ..." (Methodist Hymn Book, hymn 374, verse 3).

Step 4. She combined her faith with works to manifest God's blessing: Not only did the widow have to believe that what Elisha was instructing her to do would deliver her from her current financial crisis, but she also had to bring her faith to life by her actions.

As children of God, we are often guilty of allowing that which we have committed to the Lord in faith to lay dormant in the midst of our financial crisis: James 2:26 reminds us that faith without works is dead. To manifest His blessing, God requires us to both talk the talk and walk the walk. Too often, our failure to talk and walk our faith is due to pride, or delay that leads to doubt, or fear that immobilizes us from doing what God requires in order to manifest His blessing in our lives. This was not the case with the widow. Scripture reveals that after Elisha had given her instructions, she and her children left and did exactly as he commanded.

To manifest His blessing, God requires us to both talk the talk and walk the walk

---

When one considers what Elisha had instructed her to do—"Go borrow thee vessels abroad of *all* thy neighbors ..." (2 Ki 4:3)—pride, fear, or delay could have easily been her response. Instead, she chose to be obedient and put her faith in action immediately, without questioning. I believe she and her children followed those instructions even though it meant going to ask quarrelsome neighbors, neighbors who did her wrong in the past, neighbors she know were not particularly fond of her ... Why? Elisha had instructed her to do so. In return, the Lord abundantly rewarded that test of faith through works. What have you committed unto the Lord that is lying dormant? Is it starting a business, going back to college, writing a book, recording a CD, moving to a new city, changing jobs, or distributing a product? Whatever it may be, remember to receive God's blessing; you too will have to add works to your faith if you are to manifest the financial blessing out of that which you have committed unto to him.

Step 5. She preserved her faith: A critical lesson each of us must learn is that God only acts according to His original plan. He is not in heaven changing the plan every time we call on him. Why? God's plan was not only set before the foundation of the world, but it is already accomplished. Selah! In fulfilling His plan for our lives, He will inspire us to ask in prayer that which He has already ordained to bring about, whether immediately or after a period of time has elapsed. A critical component to manifesting God's blessing in our lives is preserving our faith during those times God's plan calls for us to wait.

God only acts according to His original plan

A careful reflection on the passage of scripture from 2 Kings 4 will reveal that Elisha specifically instructed the widow to borrow vessels "abroad" of all her neighbors. The implication here is that she was not to limit her work to her immediate neighbors. Given that this widow had probably sold all she had to keep her sons from being bondsmen, I believe they had no means of transporting themselves to collect the vessels. As a result, it took some time to gather the vessels from "abroad." I believe that Elisha knew this, and in order to preserve her faith during the period of waiting, he commanded her to shut the door upon herself and her children. As she went from neighbor to neighbor, she did not linger and tell her story; she just asked to borrow the vessels and went on to the next neighbor. When she got home at night, she did not call a friend over to talk about her situation or what she was doing. The widow gathered her children and did as Elisha had commanded her—she shut the door. She repeated this routine until she had gathered all the vessels she and her children could find.

Have you preserved your faith by shutting the door, or are you telling everyone about your situation and inviting their input and seeking their direction? Too often, the latter is exactly what we do. As a result, instead of building up our faith, this tears it down by doubt and words spoken in direct opposition to the very thing we are believing God for. I want to encourage you to shut the door once you have committed unto the Lord in faith that which He has revealed as your way of escaping your financial difficulties. Tell no one about it unless the Holy Spirit gives you utterance to do so. How will you know? There will be liberty in your spirit to do so. Unless that liberty of spirit prevails, tell no one about it.

One of my favorite accounts in the Bible concerns the Shunammite woman found in 2 Kings 4:12–37. The passage records that after the Shunammite woman's son died, she took him to Elisha's room and shut the door. I believe that behind those closed doors, she committed her situation unto the Lord in faith by prayer, and He revealed that Elisha (the man of God) was her way of escape. After she left that room, she told no one about her situation until she reached the one to whom the Holy Spirit had given her liberty to speak. Her only words were the ones she spoke in confirmation of her faith: "It is well." In so doing, she preserved her faith as she waited for the miracle she believed God could perform through His servant Elisha. God honored her faith by bring her son back to life. To receive the financial blessing God has ordained for you before the foundation of the world, you too must preserve your faith by shutting your door during the time of waiting. What he did for the Shunammite woman and the widow, He will do for you.

Step 6. She looked beyond her immediate need: In 2 King 4:6, we read the following: "It came to pass, when the vessels were full, that she said unto her son, Bring me yet a vessel. And he said unto her, There is not a vessel more. And the oil stayed." I want you to note that this widow kept asking for vessels even though she knew that the oil she had gathered thus far was more than enough to pay her debt. I believe her past experience with this miracle-working God, revealed through the work of Elijah and now Elisha, informed her that she was receiving the blessing of El Shaddai, the God of plenty, the all-sufficient one. She knew from her study of the scripture with her husband, the servant of Elisha, that the blessings of the God of Abraham, Isaac, and Jacob were not only to fulfill a need but also to bless generations. There is no doubt in my mind that if she had enough vessels, the oil would still be flowing even to this day. We serve a big God; we serve an amazing God, we serve a God who can make the impossible possible. In the midst of what seemed to be an impossible situation, He asked Jeremiah this question: "Is anything too hard for the Lord?" (Jer 32:27). The answer is *no*!

Again, I encourage you, in the midst of your financial crisis, as you commit in faith that which the Lord has provided for you as your means of escape, to think big and release your imagination. In 1 Corinthians 2:9, we are reminded of the following: "Eye hath not seen, nor ear heard, neither have entered into the heart of man, the things which God had prepared for them that love him." Lastly leave room for God to surprise you. After all, we serve a God who is full of surprises.

Step 7. She sought instructions on how to use her blessing: The passage records that after the oil stopped flowing, she sought the man of God and told him what had happened. I believe she was over the moon and bubbling with excitement. Like the leper in Luke 17:15 who returned to thank Jesus after he had received his miracle, she returned to Elisha to give thanks and seek God's directions for her blessing. The Bible records that Elisha then gave specific instructions as to how she was to use her blessing: "Go, sell the oil, and pay thy debt, and live thou and thy children of the rest" (2 Ki 4:7). His instructions reflect the fact that God already knew there would be a market for the widow's product. He knew that the price she would get would be enough to pay her bills and have enough left over for her and her children to live in abundance for the rest of their lives. By seeking God's instructions, through Elisha, the widow was assured of the successful completion of the plan of God for her and her children.

Too often when we seek the Lord for help and He graciously grants it to us, we tell God thanks and go about doing what seems right in our minds and hearts. Yet the Bible warns us, "The heart is deceitful above all things and desperately wicked ..." (Jer 17:9). The result is that, at worst, we end up back in the same place we were before; at best, we appear to have outward success, but there is no joy, peace, or contentment along the paths we took. Consider this: if you cannot successfully build a house without referring to the architect's blueprints, how can you successfully accomplish God's plan for your life without consulting with its chief architect? If you are going to be truly successful after you have received your blessing, you must seek Him for direction. The widow intuitively understood this, and she therefore lived in abundance for the rest of her life. I encourage you to follow her example.

Because of her actions, this widow was able to save her sons from becoming bondsmen and enjoy financial freedom and prosperity all her life. Again, be encouraged that what God did for her, He will do for you. By following her example, you will use the key that God gave you before you were born to unlock the financial blessing He has for you to fulfill your destiny through his plan for your life. It's not too late. Again, follow the widow's example and reap the rewards.

10

Putting it all in perspective

It was September 2008, and I was in China watching a television program when the Lord suddenly began to speak to my heart, saying, **"My children are focused on the wrong things. It will soon be over, and they will have missed God's promise of eternal life."** Wow! Selah! As we come to the conclusion of this book, it is so important to remember that God's ultimate plan for your life is not about financial wealth or financial security. It's about your preparation to receive the fullness of God's promise of eternal life.

Paul reminds us in 1 Corinthians:

> *For no one can lay any other foundation than the one we already have in Jesus Christ. Now anyone who build on that foundation may use gold, silver, jewels, wood, hay, or straw. But there is going to come a time of testing at the judgement day to see what kind of work each builder has done. Everyone's work will be put through the fire to see whether or not it keeps its value. If the work survives the fire, that builder will receive a reward. But if the work is burned up, the builder will suffer great loss. The builders themselves*

will be saved, but like someone escaping through a wall of flames (1 Cor 3:11–15, NLT).

In this passage, Paul is giving us a preview of what it will be like on Judgment Day. On that day, all of our work, including our motivations for doing the work, will be brought back before each of us to be tested by fire to see what kind of work it is. If it is made up of hay, straw, or wood, you will suffer great loss. By contrast, if your work is made up of gold, silver, or jewels, it will remain , and you will receive a reward.

I want you to pay close attention to the fact that Paul gives two scenarios that will take place on that day. The first scenario is revealed when Paul says, "For no one can lay any other foundation than the one we already have in Jesus Christ. Now anyone who builds on that foundation …" In this passage of scripture, Paul reveals a prerequisite for being tested. That prerequisite is accepting Jesus Christ as your personal Lord and Savior. If you read the scripture carefully, you will come to the understanding that it is upon Jesus that the builder builds. You and I are the builders, and if we are not building on Jesus Christ, all the work that we have accomplished during our lives, no matter how great or noble in the sight of man, will not qualify to be tested. Why? It was not built on Jesus Christ.

Paul reminds us that it is by grace that we are saved through faith; and not of ourselves: it is a gift from God: Not of works, least any man should boast (Eph 2:8–9). I want to emphasize a point that no one reading this book must miss. None of us are going to enter heaven without first accepting Jesus Christ as our personal Lord and Savior. Jesus Himself declared, "I am the way, the truth, and the life: no man cometh unto the Father but by me" (John 14:6). You cannot get there through works, no matter how religious they appear on the surface. You can't get there by being in the choir, leading the youth group, cleaning the church, being the pastor's assistant, being a local preacher, handing out leaflets, being a vestry member, helping out in the soup kitchen, leading youth fellowship, visiting the prison, or being a class leader, a steward, or a deacon. Unless you first accept Jesus Christ as your personal Lord and Savior, your work will automatically be rejected on that day.

The second scenario revolves around those who have accepted Jesus Christ as their personal Lord and Savior and have set about being laborers together with God in building on the foundation of Christ Jesus (1 Cor 3:9). As we build, Paul warns that every man should take heed how he builds on the foundation, for not everything he constructs there will be accepted (1 Cor 3:10). I believe that the works that will withstand the test of fire and receive the reward Paul speaks about will come out of those works that God has preordained for each of us to perform before the foundation of the world. The reward for Jeremiah will be given because of the work he was ordained to perform as a prophet unto the nations (Jer 1:5). The reward for Moses will come out of his preordained role as the one chosen to lead the children of Israel out of Egypt. (Ex 3:11). The reward for Peter and Paul will come out of their labor as apostles unto the Jews and Gentiles, respectively (Gal 2:7–8). How will you know the work that you have been ordained to perform? Like each of the Patriarchs named, you will feel compelled to do the work assigned to you. In his writings to the Corinthians, Paul said, "For preaching the Good News is not something I can boast about. I am compelled by God to do it!" (1 Cor 9:16, NLT).

For each of us today, the works that will withstand the test of fire will be those that fall within the plan of God for our lives. In order for us to complete those works successfully, God has provided all the financial resources needed through our obedience to the principle of tithing as administered by the Holy Spirit living within us. When we apply those financial resources to the accomplishment of the plan of God, the works we perform will withstand the test of fire, and we will receive the fullness of the reward God has for each of us.

The problem for many of God's children is that their primary focus is not on completing the plan of God for their lives. Instead, they are busy with their own agendas of fulfilling earthly desires such as wealth accumulation, business success, career advancement, and all manner of material things. The problem with these earthly pursuits, outside the plan of God for your life, is that they constitute wood, stubble, and hay in the sight of the Lord. Paul reveals that this builder will suffer loss as they are burnt on that day. The loss referred to by Paul is the loss of reward for faithful and dedicated service in completing His plan for our lives.

For those Christians who live their life with little or no dedication of service toward the fulfilling of the plan of Jesus for their lives, Paul further reveals that they "shall be saved; yet so as by fire" (1 Cor 3:15).

Let me try to give you an insight to what Paul is referring to. My family and I attended the inauguration ceremonies for President Obama in Washington, D.C., in the freezing cold. An alarm went off in our hotel in the early hours of the morning before the ceremony. The alarm was loud and persistent, and it was accompanied by the hotel guard knocking on doors, urging everyone to leave everything behind and vacate the hotel as quickly as possible. When we arrived at the bottom of the stairs, I looked around and realized that most guests had only their pajamas they went to sleep in. Had there been a fire, they would have been saved, but they would have suffered loss.

Paul is saying that on that day, there will be those who stand before Jesus and the only thing they will be able to present to Him is the fact that they have accepted Jesus Christ as their personal Lord and Savior. None of their work or only a small portion of their work will be able to withstand the test of fire that will be applied, and they shall suffer loss.

Remember, as we go about our faithful execution of God's plan for our lives, the Bible reminds us in 1 Timothy 6:19 that we are "laying up in store for [ourselves] a good foundation against the time to come, that [we] may lay hold on eternal life." The unlocking of God's financial blessing for your life is about receiving the financial resources necessary to accomplish the plan of God for your life so that you may lay hold on eternal life in all its fullness. I love what Paul said at the end of completing the plan of God for his life: "There is laid up for me a crown of righteousness, which the Lord, the righteous judge, shall give me at that day ..." (2 Tim 4:8).

The unlocking of God's financial blessing for your life is about receiving the financial resources necessary to accomplish the plan of God for your life

---

What is truly inspiring about Paul's life is that he was able to accomplish God's plan after spending the early part of his life persecuting Jesus

(Act 9:4). Be encouraged by Paul's story, for it's not too late to begin your race and finish your course.

I have a younger brother who has lived a troubled life. Recently, he wrote to me with the joy of the Lord in his heart, proclaiming that he had given his life to Jesus, saying that life would never be the same. My heart was filled with joy as I read his testimony of triumph over the adversary and the hope of eternal life to come that sprang forth from his confession. I believe that if each of us grabs hold of the eternal blessings that are bound up in unlocking God's financial blessing for our lives, we will apply all that we have learnt in this book with diligence and enthusiasm.

The Time to Begin Is Now!

David came to a revolutionary conclusion at the end of his life when he acknowledged this: "For we are strangers before thee, and sojourners, as were all our fathers: our days on the earth are as a shadow, and there is none abiding" (1 Chr 29:15). The sudden passing of my eldest brother to a heart attack was a stark reminder of this reality.

As with David, our reflection should be that life is short. We must therefore work the work of Him who sent (Jesus) and be busy with His business while it is still daylight. The Bible reminds us that night is coming on, when no man can work (John 9:4, AMP). Without work, there can be no "Well done, good and faithful servant."

Our work begins with the understanding that God has a plan for each of our lives, a mission that each of us was uniquely equipped to accomplish before the foundation of the world. In carrying out His plan, each of us can be assured that:

- The plan is under the divine protection of God himself. No harm or affliction will come upon you from which you cannot be delivered and emerge triumphant (Ps 34:19).

- The plan is detailed. Nothing has been left out of the plan. Remember, the God we serve is the alpha and omega, the beginning and the ending (Rev 1:8). He has already seen the plan accomplished and is satisfied that nothing has been left out. The final work to be completed is already beautiful in His eyes and worthy of the congratulatory remark "Well done, good and faithful servant."

- The plan makes provision for a work to be done. Concerning his work, Paul, in his letter to the Corinthians said this: "How terrible for me if I didn't do it!" (1 Cor 9:16, NLT). I believe that Paul was referring to the loss of reward he would suffer on that day if he did not do the work that God had ordained him to do. Here is the revelation in Paul's letter to the Corinthians: your reward is tied to completing the work God has ordained for you to do before the foundation of the world.

- The plan has made provision for all the resources needed to accomplish it. Whatever your needs are along the pathway to fulfilling the plan of God for your life have already been met. I believe the key to unlocking the resources necessary to successfully complete God's plan for your life is to cheerfully allow the Holy Spirit to administer the principle of tithing as reflected in the Bible and discussed in this book. God's promise is that He will open the windows of heaven and pour you out a blessing, that there shall not be room enough to receive it (Mal

3:10). Among the blessings is all the financial resources you will need to complete God's plan to the glory of His name.

Our work continues with the knowledge that we become partners with God in accomplishing His plan for our lives by accepting Jesus Christ as our personal Lord and Savior. The power and strength of that partnership is manifested through our obedience and observance of God's statutes, commandments, and ordinances in faith, by the inspiration and assistance of the Holy Spirit in our lives. It is the manifestation of that power through the Holy Ghost that allows us to defeat the work of the adversary to destroy the plan of God for our lives. Remember, if God is for you, who can be against you? (Rom 8:31).

Go forth and complete the plan of God for your life with the knowledge and understanding of its eternal reward. As you begin your journey, my prayer for you is that you are strengthened and encouraged by the revelation that all you need to successfully accomplish your plan has already been provided before the foundation of the world. May God richly bless you along the way.

References

- **Comparative Study Bible**: New International Version, Amplified Version; King James Version; Updated New American Standard Bible, Zondervan Publishing House, Grand Rapids, MI, 1999

- **The King James Study Bible:** King James Version, Thomas Nelson Publishers, Nashville, TN, 1988

- **Deluxe Study Bible:** King James Version, with commentary by Ellen G. White. Distributed by Review & Herald Publishing, Hagertown, MD, 2002 ISBN: 1878951424

- **T. D. Jakes, Life Overflowing: 6 Pillars for Abundant Living,** Bethany House, Minneapolis, MN, 2000, 2008

Notes

Additional copies of this book are available through
AuthorHouse at www.authorhouse.com

You can also order directly from us
PO Box 3339
Road Town
Tortola
British Virgin Islands

Email: mmalone@hsipublications.com

Or Visit Our Web Site
www.HSIPublications.com